"Our days are marked by unprecedented confusion about manhood. Forces in our culture denigrate masculinity as 'toxic' and push a false narrative about what it means to be a man. Many in our churches have been influenced to these ideas, and as a result, many Christian men are on the sidelines in their homes and communities. In *The War on Men*, Owen Strachan speaks courageously and exposes the ways in which unbiblical worldviews vilify God's purpose for men. Our churches and communities will be safer, freer, and stronger if the men among us live out the godly vision for manhood laid out in this book."

—**Lt. Gen. (Ret.) William Boykin,** founding member of Delta Force and executive vice president of Family Research Council

"Some would observe the impact of the feminist movement and correctly correlate the cultural decline with the advancement of its cause. Simone de Beauvior, Betty Friedan, and Gloria Steinem represent hope for those who have desired to abandon traditional roles for women. Now, the fifth phase of feminism is attempting to eradicate all gender distinctions. But the assault against masculinity began long before Beauvior, Friedan, and Steinem. Owen Strachan takes us back to the beginning of the biblical text to the core of the war on men and lays out an important foundational piece for us all to consider as we focus on Christ. If you're looking for a manual to rebuild men, this is it."

—**Virgil Walker,** executive director of operations at G3 and cohost of the *Just Thinking* podcast

"Today, the forces of woke culture, militant feminism, and androgyny are making a full-frontal assault on biblical manhood and masculinity. The war on men is real and unrelenting, but here is a book that will arm them for the fight. Here is a clear, compelling, and convictional vision of the distinction between men and women, the distinct calling and character of biblical manhood, and the necessity of maintaining these distinctions. In a world that is churning out men without chests, here is a book that will put some proverbial [theological] hairs back on our chests as men. Buy this book, buy into the truth of this book, and sell it not."

—**Philip De Courcy,** pastor of Kindred Community Church, Anaheim Hills, California, and teacher on the daily radio program *Know the Truth*

"Biblical manhood is under vicious assault as never before. Radical feminism is rampant, while passive masculinity is spreading like a malignant tumor. Society, the Church, and families are being devastated. This book by Owen Strachan, *The War on Men*, takes significant and decisive steps to point us back in the right direction. Not only does Strachan make the right diagnosis, he prescribes the medicine for the cure. Read this book."

—**Steven J. Lawson,** president of OnePassion Ministries, professor at the Master's Seminary, teaching fellow at Ligonier Ministries, and lead preacher at Trinity Bible Church of Dallas

"Those of my generation remain astonished that books defending the goodness of manhood, the rightness of God's design in creation, would have to be written. But any boy in today's world is constantly under attack, and hence needs a biblical grounding in the goodness of manhood and the propriety of masculinity. Owen Strachan's work provides exactly what is needed to provide that biblical foundation."

—**James White,** director of Alpha and Omega Ministries, professor of church history and apologetics at Grace Bible Theological Seminary

"Satan is on the warpath, seeking to destroy everyone who bears the image of God—men, women, and children. And increasingly, that war has its crosshairs set on men and masculinity. But God designed men, and while we recognize sin distorts everything, masculinity in itself is a good thing. I'm thankful for Owen's bold and powerful defense of biblical manhood. It's much needed today!"

—**Ken Ham,** CEO of Answers in Genesis, Ark Encounter, and the Creation Museum

"This book by Owen Strachan represents a call to 'man up' in the middle of a revolution that rejects humanity's binary design, made in God's image. At the same time, Owen is sounding the alarm to rally an army of strong and godly men who would raise their voices for God in defense of a biblical manhood capable of challenging the forces of evil behind this gender ideology. In one way or another, the author is calling those of us with biblical convictions to stand in the gap at a time when many have been wrongly convinced about the need for men to be of weaker character as a way of undoing the macho figure. And yet, this book will help you see that the way to accomplish such a task is by building stronger men in the image of the most manly, courageous, decisive, determined, secure, and compassionate leader of all time: our Lord and commander-in-chief, Jesus Christ. Read this book, and get in the gap!"

—**Dr. Miguel Núñez,** senior pastor of the International Baptist Church, Santo Domingo, Dominican Republic, and founder and president of Wisdom and Integrity Ministries

"The modern disdain for men has reached a point of absurdity. It is time for some clear and rational words of common sense and transcendent insights from our Creator. Owen Strachan steps up to do just that. He tackles the pressing issues of our day in his well-researched, biblically anchored, and forthright manner. You should read this book, ponder its truths, and be willing to recalibrate your understanding of what is and what should be. May God use Strachan's writing to restore our sanity, strengthen our hearts, and embolden our mouths to speak out as we fearlessly push back against this raging war on men."

—**Mike Fabarez,** author of *Raising Men, Not Boys,* and pastor of Compass Bible Church, Aliso Viejo, California

"From the very beginning, God has planned to raise up faithful and fearless men. Men are called to be faithful to God and fear nothing and no person other than Him. Our progressive and God-denying culture seeks to strip men of their manliness and raise up a new generation of feminized men who are weak and fearful. Such men become puppets of society rather than courageous God-worshipers who faithfully serve God in all spheres of life. Owen Strachan does a great job of encouraging men to remain faithful to their calling and to refuse to repent of their manliness."

—**Dr. Josh Buice,** pastor of Pray's Mill Baptist Church, Douglasville, Georgia, founder and President of G3 Ministries, and assistant professor of preaching at Grace Bible Theological Seminary

"I labored with Owen Strachan in the early 2010s to defend God's design through our work with the Council on Biblical Manhood and Womanhood. We saw the cultural downgrade then that has led to the unmitigated catastrophe that is today's gender chaos. In many ways, this book is the fruit of his insightful thinking on the subject for the past decade. It is a wonderful antidote to the madness, especially for Christian men. It serves as a clarion call to 'act like men.' To be brave for Christ. To live for God's honor. To renew a biblical vision for God's 'grand design' for masculinity, as Strachan has so often put it. Lives will be changed for God's glory as a result of this vision, and for that, I rejoice."

    —**Grant Castleberry,** senior pastor of Capital Community Church, Raleigh, North Carolina, and founder and president of Unashamed Truth Ministries

"Over the past decade, no one I know has studied more thoroughly, written more clearly, or spoken more boldly and passionately on the issue of manhood than Dr. Owen Strachan. His superb book *The War on Men* comes not only as a cultural and philosophical analysis of the current attack on manhood, but also as a convicting and inspiring biological and biblical study on what manhood acutely is and how the Gospel saves and transforms men. Written in an accessible style with practical helps, this searching work is a must-read in our day—and any day. May it be used to point many to the great need of the hour: men of God. Men like Christ."

    —**Gavin Peacock,** author of *A Greater Glory* and associate pastor of Calvary Grace Church of Calgary, Alberta, Canada

"If you don't understand what's going on in our world today, read this book! Our godless culture wants men weak, hesitant, soft, compliant, and safe. That way, we won't engage, unite, and fight back against the Marxist revolution we are all in. If you want to change the direction, this book diagnoses the problem and gives the solution. It's one word: men! Strong men. Manly men. Real men. Christlike men. If that's not you, read this book. If that is you, read it with a man who isn't. Become countercultural through the teachings in this book, and watch as your life flourishes with the joy, fulfillment, and clarity that comes from being who God designed and saved you to be. Strong men are anything but toxic. They are a blessing to a godly wife, a family, the Church, and society, and they are the last line of defense in a dying culture. Dr. Strachan has done us all a huge favor by being willing to take the attacks that will come from writing this book. So men, read it, and you'll be equipped for the (so far mostly nonviolent) civil war you're already in."

—**Jon Benzinger,** lead pastor of Redeemer Bible Church, Gilbert, Arizona, and author of *Stand*

"This book will hit the androgyny-loving culture and her disciple, the feminist evangelical church, like a stone to Goliath's forehead. Dripping with Scripture and full of up-to-date research, Dr. Strachan's book rightly diagnoses the problems facing men in the West and dishes out the biblical cure: salvation, restoration, and reformation through the God-Man. He tells of Jesus's example for men, good news for men, and His commission for men without any backpedaling or virtue-signaling. He is honest about the current dire situation, but his battle plan provides hope for those who can bear to hear what God's Word says. Accessible and tremendously profitable for any man."

—**Thomas Foord,** pastor of Hope Reformed Baptist Church, Queensland, Australia, and president of Fellowship of Evangelical Churches of Australia

"The society we live in today continues to blur the lines between men and women, attempting to deconstruct everything we know by nature to be true about both genders, much to society's ongoing demise. The solution is simple, but not easy: we must embrace the reality of who we are and how we are to function, and there's no better way to do so than through God's Word. *The War on Men* lays out several examples of the issues we face today and then goes to God's Word to unearth many models of biblical masculinity, including the perfect example in the Lord Jesus Christ. Strachan avoids the trap of embracing flawed, worldly views of masculinity while also avoiding the opposite error of making manhood an exclusively spiritual issue. While the book clearly focuses on men, there is much to recommend to everyone of both genders. Understanding the biblical arguments made will equip everyone not only to embrace God's unique design for each gender, but to reject the many ways the world seeks to undermine what God deems good."

—**Ekkie Tepsupornchai,** senior pastor of Western Avenue Baptist Church, Brawley, California

"Owen Strachan knows that the challenges facing men and boys are not simply cultural and societal, but spiritual and theological, and has written a challenging and bracing book in defense of the goodness of God-given masculinity. Although his assertions will undoubtedly infuriate many who resist any positive vision of traditional and spiritual masculinity, it will nevertheless be a welcomed tonic for the beleaguered, confused, and often maligned men who are attempting to exist in a culture in which being a man is considered a liability rather than a responsibility. As a son, a husband, a pastor, and the father of three future men (and two future women!), I am grateful for the necessary, timeless, and enduring reminder of the loving and profound ways that God has designed and called men to His work, service, and witness to the world."

—**Rev. Dr. John D. Koch Jr.**, rector of Saint Luke's Anglican Church, Hilton Head Island, South Carolina

THE WAR ON MEN

THE WAR ON MEN

Why Society Hates Them and
Why We Need Them

OWEN STRACHAN

SALEM
BOOKS
an imprint of Regnery Publishing
Washington, D.C.

Salem Books™ is a trademark of Salem Communications Holding Corporation.
Regnery® and its colophon are registered trademarks of Salem Communications Holding Corporation.

Cataloging-in-Publication data on file with the Library of Congress.

ISBN: 978-1-68451-445-8
eISBN: 978-1-68451-474-8

Published in the United States by
Salem Books
An Imprint of Regnery Publishing
A Division of Salem Media Group
Washington, D.C.
www.SalemBooks.com

Manufactured in the United States of America

10 9 8 7 6 5 4 3 2 1

Books are available in quantity for promotional or premium use. For information on discounts and terms, please visit our website: www.SalemBooks.com.

To Grant Castleberry,

a dear friend and faithful man who lives for the honor of God alone

CONTENTS

CONTENTS

Foreword

My friendship with Owen Strachan was forged in fire. We met amid an ideological battle that was tearing the Church (and the culture) apart. Both of us were on what appeared to be the losing side, but neither of us was willing to yield. Instead, we fought like men! At the end of the day, it doesn't matter whether we won or lost. In fact, that battle is still raging, and we are still fighting. What really matters is that we both decided to fight. The book you hold in your hands is Owen's latest salvo. In today's feminized, confused, antimasculine world, that is enough to get us both labeled as toxic men. That's why this book is so important.

Men really are under fire. Words like "fight," "war," "battle," and "debate" are frowned upon these days because of their masculine underpinnings. We have been conditioned to view manliness and everything associated with it as inherently dangerous and destructive. Consequently, we are raising a generation of men who are ashamed of being men. The result is men who are caricatures—what C. S. Lewis called "men without chests." Many modern men are either hypermasculine or effeminate. There is no sense of balance. It seems the only men who can win the approval of the culture today are the ones who decide they are actually women. Hence, Lia Thomas, Dylan Mulvaney, and Caitlyn Jenner are given awards while masculine men are vilified on the big screen, pilloried in the press, and run off college campuses.

This book is important because men really are not toxic. When a building is on fire, a gunman is on the loose, or someone is being robbed or beaten and men rush in to face the danger, no one argues that they are being toxic. Why? Because deep down, we know that God designed men for such tasks. Men are rough, rugged, risk-taking creatures from their earliest days. Boys are always looking for things to jump off of or ways to make things go faster and higher. They are constantly looking for things (or people) to crash into. All of this is both a natural expression of the way God made us and preparation for moments in life when the courage, determination, and willingness to risk that we forge in boyhood is called upon because the world needs men—real men. Men who go to war. Men who go to the moon. Men who take wives and love them, build homes and maintain them, and raise, protect, and provide for children. Far from being toxic, men are essential.

This book is important because God loves manhood...and so should we. Manhood is part of God's design. In the beginning, God "made them male and female" (Genesis 1:27). The differences between men and women are as beautiful and glorious as they are necessary. God designed men on purpose and with a purpose. God sanctified and honored manhood by revealing Himself through His Word, using terms and metaphors like "Father," "Son," and "husband." Thus, when we malign manhood, we malign God Himself. Moreover, we create a vacuum where men are supposed to be—and nature, abhorring a vacuum, is more than happy to fill that space with inadequate, worldly, and Satanic substitutes.

This book is important because men need the grace and mercy of God to reclaim and reassert their manhood in today's antimasculine world. One of the most unfortunate aspects of the war on men is that boys are discouraged from becoming men in any real sense. Men are condemned and even punished for exhibiting masculinity. Now an entire generation doesn't know what manhood is supposed to look like. Men walk away from the responsibilities of marriage and fatherhood, they can't or won't hold down jobs, and many spend more time playing video games than they do engaged in any meaningful endeavor. And the results are catastrophic!

When men are absent, families suffer. When men are weak, women suffer. When men are immature and irresponsible, children suffer. And when men are too blind to see the havoc that their absence, weakness, immaturity, and irresponsibility wreaks, the entire society suffers. That's why we need books like this to point us to the only hope men have ever had: the God who made us. This is not a time to sit and sulk about the war on men. This is the time to heed David's words to his son, Solomon, and "Be strong and courageous and do it. Do not be afraid and do not be dismayed, for the LORD GOD, even my God, is with you. He will not leave you or forsake you…" (1 Chronicles 28:20).

—**Voddie Baucham Jr.,**
dean of the School of Divinity at African Christian University
in Lusaka, Zambia, and the author of the bestseller *Fault Lines*
(Salem Books, 2021)

Introduction

Never yield to force; never yield to the apparently overwhelming might of the enemy.

Winston Churchill

Masculinity is toxic.

Just three words long, this poisonous little sentence captures the spirit of our age. Painting with broad strokes, traditional manhood and strong manhood are problematic, deeply problematic. Risk-taking, aggressiveness, compartmentalizing to focus on tasks, enduring hardship without emoting, being stoic, conflict, war, manliness in general: all this is bad, essentially. Whether religious or not, if you are drawn to most anything in the previous sentence (especially if you're a man), you are very likely a part of the problem that ails society. In the most succinct form: You're participating in the culture of "toxic masculinity."

In general terms, elite American culture today despises manhood. This is especially true of what I call "strong manhood" of the spiritual and traditional kind. Too often, when men show strength, even virtuously, leftist voices shame them. Such men are *toxic*. Men who fall into this category are not good; they are not the very backbone of society. Christians see strong men as the *solution* to our earthly struggles, at least many of them (empowered by God's grace). Our pagan culture, by contrast, sees strong men as the *problem*.[1]

So comes the dreaded label: "You're acting out your toxicity!" The only tolerated response to this charge is embracing it. But mark this well: when you fall prey to the culture and tell people you're *toxic*, you sign a living death warrant. You enter the therapeutic Matrix, a dystopian place you'll never truly leave. There is no Gospel in this worldview; there is no redemption; there is no forgiveness; there is no Christ. There is only you as a man owning your privilege and renouncing your power. But not just this: You will renounce any notion of manhood itself. The new paganism will tolerate no hard-and-fast notions of the sexes. All will bow to this unrealism.

The new paganism is a vision of the world that sees all that exists as "one." There is no Creator; there is only the divinized human person, and we may do—sexually and otherwise—whatever we wish. The new paganism that dominates our age is not communal. The new paganism is strikingly imperial. When you embrace this evil ideology, you will not be left to your own devices. No, the regime will come for you, and swiftly.

It will not come to affirm you; affirmation exists in full and flowing measure for the LGBTQIA folks, those who find their identity in their fallen desires, those who reject the moral and social order instituted by God. Do not be mistaken: The gender activists get the gold star, but strong men get the iron rod. All this is "justice"; all this is *intersectional*. Having dominated Western society for centuries, it's time for men to lose in the great power games of life, and lose big.

This losing will not be theoretical. You as a man will lose. Led by gender theorists, outspoken celebrities, leftist politicians, and secular therapists, you will unlearn traditional manhood. You will break with religious doctrine that dares to tell men to "act like men" and "man up." You will embrace your "feminine side." You will stop seeking to be strong; you will embrace being soft. You will step back so strong women can lean in. You will learn to love androgyny, blur your gender, queer your sex, and live not according to God's design, but pagan lies.

As you unlearn your toxicity, your entire way of thinking and living will change. You will shift from a traditional outlook, with its emphasis on chivalry and self-denial and courage for men, into a thoroughly postmodern one. You will not protect women; you will not try to stop physically robust adult men from entering restrooms where unprotected little girls are changing their clothes; you will not stand against body-ravaging surgeries that facilitate a "gender transition"; you will not raise your son or daughter in any sex-specific way; you will not speak or think as if there is anything traditionally identified as manly or womanly at all. You will defame all such thinking and repent of all such practices.

If you are a Christian, you will stop referring to God as "Father," and you'll switch that referent to "Mother." You will celebrate women as the lead voices in local churches and Christian organizations, you will work with all haste to platform female preachers, and you will curse out loud the idea that there is any "creation order" that calls men to self-sacrificial yet genuinely authoritative leadership.

All this is vital to the ongoing revolution. Christians must be thoroughly and holistically reeducated. They must give up their stubborn belief in men being appointed as the teachers and elders and preachers of the Church as those made first by God, and thus fashioned for leadership by divine design (as based on 1 Timothy 2:9–15). It is the Church, after all, that historically stands as the last bulwark against ungodly evil—but if the Church itself can be transformed, then the pagan revolution will move yet faster.

Welcome to the War on Men

In all this, you will bow the knee to the new pagan ideology, or you will pay the severest price imaginable. You will never leave your therapeutic reconditioning; instead, in the most Orwellian and Huxleyan way, you will exist in this therapeutic netherworld, this anti-reality dystopia, until the day you depart this earth. You will be rewired, reprogrammed, and rendered something decidedly less than a man. Welcome to the war on truth. Welcome to the war on Scripture. Welcome to the war on the sexes.

And yes: Welcome to the war on men.

Do not be confused, however. The war that I have just outlined (and that you are already acquainted with) is not fought on an actual battlefield. Neither is it a fair war or what you could call a "good war"—one waged on equal terms. Instead, it is a war waged by keyboard, by soundbite, by fevered classroom indoctrination. In the public square, the classroom, Hollywood, and other environs influenced by leftist and Marxist ideology, manhood is under fire. Alongside the popular charge of "toxic masculinity," consider such common mantras and statements as these, all of which boys and young men hear today:

The future is female.

Smash the patriarchy.

Gender is a construct.

Wanting to be "manly" is ridiculous.

Those repeating such mantras in political, educational, and entertainment contexts not only declare verbal war on manhood: They raise high the flag of androgyny. They sing loudly from the hymnal of fluidity. They celebrate those who bend their gender and "queer" their identity.

Broadly speaking, our culture now actively champions the inverse of nature, the reversal of what is good. In terms of hairstyles and broader physical presentation, many men now look like women, and many women look like men. Cursing the "binary," both sexes embrace the blur of androgyny. As an illustration, we find ourselves increasingly surrounded by "man-buns" and the "skittle-hair" trend, as on many campuses one finds young women (and men) sporting blunt chopped hair dyed orange or green or purple, a nose ring, or other piercings in their ears (or other places). To a troubling degree, universities and increasingly high schools seem to have become parallel-gender universes, where the twoness of man and woman has been replaced with a spectrum of fluid flexibility.

You could summarize the trends this way: In our time, defined manhood is bad, and defined womanhood is bad. Bodily clarity is out; bodily confusion is in. By pedagogy and intention, manhood and womanhood blur into one another. In the main, androgyny has replaced the binary.

This is not accidental; this is intentional.

On Joyce Carol Oates

I realized that there was a war against men not long ago. As a theology professor who has worked for years in the field of manhood, I sometimes speak at conferences and churches. Even when speaking at a church that was trying to train men in biblical manhood, I grew accustomed to people snickering, and even laughing out loud, at the word "manly." I would use it in my sermons and messages without irony, but people would nonetheless laugh at this seemingly untroubling adjective. No doubt one reason why is summed up by Harvard professor Harvey Mansfield: "Manliness is an exclusion of women but a reproach to men, to unmanly men."[2]

Mansfield nailed the target—and knew of what he wrote, having been an early lightning rod in the recent gender wars of the last twenty years or so. The term "manly" was itself a reproach, because so many men were unmanly. To them, the idea of conduct, dress, appearance, speech, and comportment that was distinctly masculine was ridiculous. Such thinking was a holdover from a bygone era, an embarrassing worldview promoting traditional gender roles that Hollywood, the media, the feminist academy, and mainstream culture had spent decade upon decade burning to ash.

But some will snort at what I have so far argued. Encountering such a view, they might respond in disbelief, *Men are under attack? I thought you were a serious person! Men have only dominated human history for millennia and are just now suffering the slightest loss of power, and so they scream and whine like little babies.* For some, the very suggestion that men are embattled will itself reinforce the perception of "toxic" male mindsets.

There is a certain logic to this case. (Indeed, it's basically a Kafka trap, in which you are guilty no matter what you do or say.) But if one pays attention, we do indeed see a battle raging over the nature of men in our time. For example, esteemed writer Joyce Carol Oates made international headlines when she tweeted: "…straight white males is the only category remaining for villains & awful people in fiction & film & popular culture. 'Bet you'll miss us when we're gone.'"[3]

Oates is not exactly on the shortlist for speakers on the men's-conference circuit. For voicing such an observation, she reaped the gentle tones and nuanced commentary of the Twitter hordes, as these replies show:

"Your early work was fantastic but I think it's time people check you into a retirement home."

"no we think you're a villain for using your platform to spout republican talking points. And writing blonde!"

"Joyce what are you even saying"

Whatever one thinks of Oates's argument, she certainly touched a nerve.

Nor was she alone in speaking to the perception of manhood in our time. Not long afterward, *Avatar* director James Cameron made international headlines by declaring testosterone "dangerous." Reflecting on his film catalogue, which includes *The Terminator* franchise, he said,

> A lot of things I did earlier, I wouldn't do—career-wise and just risks that you take as a wild, testosterone-poisoned young man. I always think of [testosterone] as a toxin that you have to slowly work out of your system.[4]

This formulation drew interest for several reasons, not least because Cameron equated testosterone with poison. In his estimation, testosterone is terminated.

These comments are in line with the American Psychological Association's shocking 2019 ruling on "traditional masculinity." The leading secular psychological authority, which has worldwide influence, has taken steps to normalize same-sex attraction and homosexual identity. In similar terms, "traditional masculinity ideology," an APA report declared,

> has been shown to limit males' psychological development, constrain their behavior, result in gender role strain and gender role conflict and negatively influence mental health and physical health.[5]

Moreover, the report said, masculinity ideology stands as

> a particular constellation of standards that have held sway over large segments of the population, including: antifemininity, achievement, eschewal of the appearance of weakness, and adventure risk and violence.[6]

This body of thought causes boys to live by a code of "suppressing emotions and masking distress." The conclusion the APA registered rings out clear as a bell: "traditional masculinity—marked by stoicism, competitiveness, dominance and aggression—is, on the whole, harmful."[7]

Clearly, the APA has declared war on manhood. There is no other conclusion we can draw. Much that the West has traditionally valued, and that the Bible in appropriate form teaches and celebrates, the APA and numerous outlets, institutions, and cultural leaders now oppose in the sharpest fashion. The line in the sand is drawn, and the battle against "traditional masculinity" advances. Few now dare to speak on men's behalf.

The Rise of Masculine Women and Feminine Men

A new gender order has arisen to take the place of the old one. Increasingly, the sexes no longer live out traditional scripts. In our strange new world, women are the empowered ones. Though feminism was first queered and has lately gone trans, a strong residue of girl-power ideology remains in our world. Generally, girls are encouraged to speak up, and loudly. They are increasingly being depicted as the heroes in our movies and shows. Theirs is the career that drives their marriage and family. In such a setting, men are urged to take on the traditional wifely role of support.

All too often, men weep easily, share their feelings uninhibitedly, speak nasally, think maternally, walk mincingly, talk haltingly, and engage others passive-aggressively. Men, per our culture, regularly "become" women now. Sure, there is some discomfort when young men identifying as female enter women's restrooms and locker rooms. But even such invasiveness draws relatively little comment from many thought leaders—indeed, those who speak out against it are usually demonized for not being "on the right side of history." Women first asked to take the place of men, and as feminism has succeeded culturally, they did; now men reciprocate by asking to be received as women, and largely are.

Many boys and young men know they do not fit into this new paradigm, though they may not understand everything that swirls around them, demanding they confess their toxicity and abandon their ingrained masculinity. In startling measure, theirs is a confused and confusing existence—one that rarely coheres, rarely makes sense, and rarely yields fulfillment and understanding.

Opposition to training in godly manhood proliferates today. We have many critics, but few who speak up to define what must be defined and defend what must be defended. In such a context, young men who genuinely want to understand their identity and duties have little help today. Many languish. They have lost the script, as Richard Reeves notes: "Many men are left feeling dislocated. Their fathers and grandfathers had a pretty clear path to follow: work, wife, kids. But what now?"[8]

As with young men, so with many young women. For a sizeable number, the traditional path to maturity and joy is gone. We can observe numerous troubling trends in a range of categories. In terms of patterns, for example, marriage is delayed. Family-building is delayed. Vocational fulfillment is stifled. Much of what gives life meaning and substance is on hold. In this vacuum, synthetic experiences abound. Instead of a real wife, young men consume pornographic videos with imaginary partners. Instead of a real family, young men spend copious amounts of time with their friend group—their "framily." Instead of embracing maturity, young men prolong their adolescence, chasing pretend adventures on big-screen TVs and computers. Instead of building a vocation, young men either evade work or bounce from job to job.

For a growing number of our young, the script is indeed lost. In disconcerting measure, young men suffer—and young women suffer with them.[9] Meanwhile, different elements of our culture aid and abet these ill developments. Behind it, an even darker force applauds—the real devil that seeks to destroy men and all image-bearers made by God, that labors to ensnare young men in a pretend world ruled by lies instead of the real world enchanted by the Creator.

The Peterson Phenomenon: A Father in Public

In dire straits, with few guides at hand, many young men have turned to the internet for help. In general terms, the strongest voice advocating for some form of strong manhood has been the intellectual Jordan Peterson. When he simultaneously refused to use the new gender vocabulary and then went on to provide practical instruction in adulthood and resilience some five to seven years ago, he started to become a cultural touchstone. Dressed to the nines, looking dapper and distinguished, speaking at times with a sharp and forceful voice, here was that lost and forgotten figure—the father—emerging from nowhere to offer strong and clear direction. Millions of young men and women alike responded positively to Peterson's program from all corners of the globe.

We can read this phenomenon from different angles, to be sure. In the simplest terms, Peterson was willing to be a father in public, essentially, unafraid of challenging the lies of LGBT ideology even as he offered the rising generation the gifts of common-sense wisdom and a form of parental attention. These have fallen into short supply as the West has lost its Judeo-Christian moorings amidst the neo-pagan and Marxist takeover of institutions. Though not a born-again believer, Peterson showed real courage in a traditionally masculine way by opposing falsehood. In doing so, he put his career on the line and won much respect.

It is tragic that Peterson and the other influencers mentioned above have in many cases proven more willing to say hard truths than many shepherds of God's flock. Too often, the leaders of Christ's Church have proven unwilling to address "controversial" subjects. If the left problematizes an area in our time, making a subject off-limits (like manhood, for example), some Christian leaders react by going quiet about it in an effort to be seen as "winsome."

This is exactly the wrong move. When the culture makes biblical wisdom "controversial," we should speak to it. We should clarify what is true and what is a lie, doing so in love and not hatred (Ephesians 4:15). We should shepherd the sheep to understand God's standard and measure it against the counterfeit. Doing so is not "culture war," though it may be called that. Doing so is offering the people of God spiritual protection so that they are not taken captive by demonic systems (Colossians 2:8; 2 Corinthians 10:3-6).

In a culture that wars against manhood, this means boys need both biblical teaching and practical training. Boys and young men certainly need to know how God defines manhood. That is of first importance. But learning does not stop with biblical study; boys need wisdom about all sorts of things that may not be explicitly covered in Scripture. They also need to know how to talk to a girl. They need to know how to dress. They need to know how to hold a mature conversation. They need to know how to change a tire. They need to know how to avoid the trap of pride but also the trap of becoming effeminate. They do not know these things, in many cases, and they may well have no godly father figure to teach them in an atmosphere of Christian discipleship.

So, as mentioned above, young men turn to voices who will speak to these matters. Hungry for truth and practical wisdom, they lurk on Reddit boards about ignored elements of the masculine life, watch videos from "manosphere" experts, and closely observe mixed-martial artists and rappers and confident celebrities in an effort to glean what they can of strong manhood. They track Tucker Carlson's fearless monologues, binge Jocko Willink podcasts, listen in on Joe Rogan's extended (and often surprisingly vulnerable) conversations with male guests, track how David Goggins spends his time, and embrace the rugged fitness ethic of Cameron Hanes.

No doubt the content produced by these figures draws an audience because, in some cases, they are worldly and exciting. But in other cases, these leaders are popular and followed the globe over because young men hunt wisdom. They need practical answers to the questions their developing masculinity presents. Yet frequently, the figures of yesterday who would have given such counsel—pastors, engaged fathers, coaches, teachers, and so on—no longer do so. In all too many cases, such men are attacked, beaten down, embittered, or absent. Ours is increasingly a fatherless age; in such sad days, young men make YouTube personalities their functional authority figure.

Deficient Manhood vs. Strong Manhood

The young men who are not being trained—and in Christian terms, not being discipled as godly men—do not stay boys. They grow up, at least in age. When they do so, if they have not been nurtured and cared for, they struggle. In fact, because of their innate physiology and wiring, they often struggle more dramatically than young women. They are already sinners, and thus are in grave need of God's saving grace. But sin mixed with blooming testosterone is a potent force that can wreak havoc on families, communities, and even the world.

In my estimation, based on my study of the Scripture and my observations, struggling men generally fall into four major categories of deficiency.

The *soft man* is one who adopts a fundamentally effeminate app-roach. He yields to the strong woman and takes his cues from her. He is still a man, but he does not display assertive or aggressive manhood. Instead, he practices a softer, more tentative masculinity, often making light of the traditional paradigm he rejects.

The *exaggerated man* encounters modern gender ideology and rejects it outright, embracing in its place a cartoonish manhood drip-ping with machismo. Foolishly, he tries to prove his manhood through physical strength, flashy wealth, and sexual promiscuity.

The *lost man* spies the confusion all around him and walks away; he abandons his duties and loved ones, ghosting all the way around.

The *angry* man takes this a step further. He not only turns away from society, but does so in wrath. His life becomes an exercise in vengeance, and all around him suffer as a result. He does not reject strength but puts it to evil use.

There is a better form of manhood than these four types: the *strong man*. This man is not strong in himself; he is strong through the power of God. He is a redeemed man, born again by the grace and mercy of his Maker. He does not live for himself, nor use his strength for selfish ends. Instead, he uses his strength for the good of others, whether physically, morally, intellectually, or spiritually. The strong man is a force for good. He is a man under discipline and a soldier under orders. He lives not by his own creed, but by the truth of God.

The strong man makes no apology for his identity. He recognizes that both by teaching and by nature, he is called to strength. He is the stronger sex, and his wife is the weaker vessel. He is called to leadership in the home, the church, and society. The leadership he is called to provide is not arbitrary but is based on the order of creation:

he was made first by God, and the woman was made from his own body. Thus the strong man, whether married (as most men will be) or single, is not made to be a lone alpha. His strength is for the good of himself and others.

The strong man is not one-sided. He is a man of many virtues and distinct vocations. This kind of man is tender with a crying daughter, firm yet loving with a foolish son, humble when confronted in his sin, quick to listen to his anxious wife, slow to anger when sinfully attacked, encouraging to the young men looking to him for help, respectful to the older men around him, disciplined with his eating and exercise, unflinching when urged to compromise his faith, gentle with a grieving friend, gracious and humble in his demeanor, moved to tears at a funeral, unflappable in the face of adversity, rough and ready for the trials of this world. Strong men, as I shall be at pains to say, are not one thing; strong men are many things.

The strong man is in no way *soft*, though he treasures women and is gentle and tender with them. The strong man cannot be *lost*, for by the grace of God he will stay at his post and honor his duties. The strong man cannot be *exaggerated*, for he does not find his worth or identity in using others and being seen in a certain light. The strong man will not become characterized by ungodly *anger*, for by the Spirit of God he kills his sin and disciplines his instincts. The strong man is the man the world is looking for but cannot find, for our culture has banished him into the wilderness. Our radical new gender order reads all strong men the same way, when in truth, masculine strength takes different forms, both for good and for ill.

Strong manhood is now seen as toxic manhood; strong men are now seen as outmoded—men who must be overcome and cancelled. We are sold this replacement—this gelded man—as a great good. It is, we are assured, a great gain for women and a great help to young men.

Unfortunately, this is a lie.

The Hero Test:
Who Produces Heroes?

The problem with our modern situation is that we still need heroes. On occasion, at least, we still need strength. We do not speak well of strong manhood, as we have seen; all too often, we deride testosterone and risk-taking and toughness. These are not seen as virtues any longer, but evils. Such ideology is promoted and celebrated in many classrooms, TV shows, and outlets: *Strong men bad; soft men allowed.*

So far, so good. But here is the problem: What about when crises happen? What about when public shooters open fire on innocent people? What about when power lines go down? What about when terrorists invade peaceable societies? What about when a woman well-versed in feminist power suffers a breakdown and cannot care for herself? What about when "work-life balance" falls apart and the family needs a provider? What about when boys act up and do not listen to the women who put them in "timeouts"? What about when false teaching begins nipping at the edges of the church family, and smooth talkers manipulate people into unsound thinking? What about when risks are called for, when aggression is needed, when evil must be ferociously resisted?

Let's give this phenomenon a name: the Hero Test. When strong or heroic action is needed, who will provide it? Or, even before a moment of panic paralyzes many, who can produce those who will show up, brave great danger, and risk their lives for others?

Some will note that both men *and* women can respond courageously, which is surely true. But as just one example, when a man of great strength, aggression, and ferocity attacks others, who will prove able to subdue him? In many crises, simply put, we need masculine strength, masculine aggression, and masculine focus. This is not because women lack courage, but because—as we shall learn from

Scripture—men have been made by God to stand down evil, shoulder hard tasks, lift heavy burdens, and tackle desperate situations, all for the good of women and children.

Beyond a shadow of a doubt, our radical new gender order cannot accomplish these aims. Truly this is the evil paradox of leftist gender education: it depends upon that which it deconstructs. Even while woke voices and gender theorists urge the revision of gender stereotypes, they still depend upon strong men to keep the lights on, plow the roads, put enemies to flight, police evil, clear debris, and keep order. This is a deep and cutting irony. The proponents of chaos need order just as much as the rest of us. But order does not keep itself; it must be tended, stewarded, and guarded. Everyone wants to be a revolutionary, but there is no revolution unless someone pays the Wi-fi bill.

You could sum up the point like this: Gender ideology does not produce heroes. It produces only those who need them but no longer have them.

Tragedy in Texas:
A Flashpoint for the Gender Wars

The Hero Test is no fantasy exercise. We recently witnessed the war over manhood surfacing in a tragic scene when a shooter named Salvador Ramos opened fire in an elementary school in Uvalde, Texas. Defying common sense and sanity itself, the local police department ordered its officers to wait outside the building while he gunned down nineteen children and two adults. It sounds like a lie, but it is the truth: grown men bearing deadly weapons, who had been trained for combat situations, just and stood outside the school for nearly an hour while massive loss of life took place inside.

The failure and cowardice on display here boggled the mind. It rightfully raised a public outcry in subsequent days. By then, however, the damage had quite literally been done. As I studied this terrible outcome, I realized that we were seeing the bitter fruit of the new gender order. Timidity, not aggression, marked the response. Great evil drew no forceful reply. Grown men did not risk their safety, but waited minute after minute, doing nothing. Instead of principled action, passive dithering carried the day. All of this came at the cost of many lives.

Yet even in this debacle, we saw a ray of hope. One man, Jacob Albarado, refused to stand still. After receiving a distress call from his wife—a teacher at the school—Albarado, an off-duty Border Patrol agent, grabbed a powerful gun and raced over immediately. Against orders, he entered the school with a few associates and began ushering children and staff members to safety. His action displayed the enduring presence of courage in this compromised situation. Yet we note carefully that Albarado had to defy the orders of his superiors in order to do what was right.

The passive officers standing many deep presented a sharp contrast to Albarado's courageous charge. Here we find the two poles of the war on men. One side sits back, neither attempting nor achieving heroism. The other side runs toward danger, risking personal safety and second-guessing from others in order to try to save lives.

In the aftermath, it was glaringly apparent that Uvalde's police department had acted in inexcusable weakness—but what was left unsaid was that such inaction and weakness fits perfectly the new paradigm on manhood. If, as the APA declared, it is bad for men to take risks, be tough, and assert themselves, then we should not be shocked when they don't. The new gender ideology deconstructs manhood, penalizes men for courage, and in so doing, makes the world a much more dangerous place than it already is.

The new gender ideology fails the Hero Test. It cannot do otherwise, for it is an ideology that rewires nature to drain men of their natural instincts.

The Way Forward for Our Study

There is a better way forward than what our culture promotes and celebrates—a much better way. Before we can grasp it, though, we need to look in greater detail at the war on men. In coming chapters, I will bring witnesses to the stand in the form of data and empirical studies that show us that boys and men in the West—primarily in America—are under fire. In Chapter 1, I show how men are struggling; Chapter 2 delves into the reasons why, as we consider different anti-male voices.

In Chapter 3, we discuss God's truth about manhood. We have a special burden in this book to understand men's distinctiveness, for the culture has gone blind to this reality and we need to recover it. We do not seek the wisdom of modern prophets, but rather visit the ancient world, studying the earth's earliest days in Genesis 1–3 to understand men's identity. Chapter 4 examines the different models of manhood, analyzing several noteworthy men from the Old Testament. Chapter 5 examines Christ—the true man—observing His multidimensional righteousness, all of which affects and shapes us.

In Chapter 6, we engage the New Testament's teaching on manhood—commands and descriptions of it, the callings of the husband, the father, the elder, and single man. We examine the physical distinctiveness of men in Chapter 7, showing that their very physiology speaks to their identity and duties. Chapter 8 traces fifteen elements of men's personal and social distinctiveness. The book concludes in Chapter 9 with a plan for training boys in the truths covered in this book, and a hopeful word for men who have stumbled and fallen into sin.

In all this, we operate by this conviction: men are not outmoded. Men are not virtueless. Men should not be cancelled. In truth, the dire situation before us today requires us to fight *for* men, not against them. This is not to excuse the real sins and failings of men, though. The solution before us is neither to coddle men nor to burn them down. It is to be honest with them and challenge them. After all, hope does not start in the land of make-believe; hope dawns when honesty speaks. Men are sinners (just like women), and as such need Jesus desperately. This applies to conversion, to becoming a Christian through faith in Christ's cross and resurrection, and to every single day of our lives as believers.

But men also need encouragement—much encouragement. They need help. They need tenderness. They need love—a lot of it. They need an arm around the shoulder. They need a father who draws them near for a regular embrace, not a stiff and awkward one. They need to hear "I love you." They need to know that they can overcome their failings. They need to know that even when they do form their own sin patterns, mercy is real and grace is powerful. Men do not need hatred and cancellation; men need investment, attention, wisdom, love, and encouragement.

Conclusion

Men should not be rewired. Men should not be broken down, shamed, and left behind by a culture dedicated to pagan lies. Men, in the simplest analysis, are *not* toxic. Men are sinners who need the redeeming blood and life-giving resurrection power of Jesus Christ. No man is hopeless; no man is without purpose; no man is too far gone for God to reach him, remake him, and put him to work.

We should not go to war against men. Nor do men need a therapeutic program by which to reengineer themselves to please the pagan power brokers of the Western left. In civility and love, but also in unyielding conviction, we must reject such poisonous ideology. We must do something far better and far more costly: We should help, train, love, correct, and rebuild men, even as we should love our boys and disciple them into biblical manhood.

Men need God. But we cannot stop there: in human terms, we desperately need men. God has staked much on them: by the order of creation, He has called them to be leaders in the home, church, and society. Without men filling the roles of husbands and fathers at home, elders in the local church, and public leaders in all sorts of contexts, all will suffer.

Strong men never will accomplish God's purposes alone, as if we do not need women. What an unsound and ungracious argument that is! The woman, from the start, is called the "helper" of man, indicating that she brings numerous gifts, abilities, and strengths to the table. Women and men are not made to compete; they are made to complement one another, and indeed they do. But that stated, if we do not have the anthropological foundation of strong manhood, the entire culture will crumble.

All this means, quite simply, that strong men are not the *problem*. As this book exists to say, strong men powered by God are the *solution*.

CHAPTER 1

How Men Are Struggling

The unhappiness of men flows directly
from the collapse of their old social role as
protectors and providers.

Roger Scruton

The young man grew up in a stable and respectable home. His family did not lack for any upper-middle-class comforts; not just anyone can own several vineyards, for example, and produce boutique white wines. Yet the home was not dedicated to fine things, at least not historically. The patriarchs had been mostly rabbis, on both sides of the family tree.

But all that changed when the government declared Jews could not serve as lawyers. When that happened, the young man's father dropped his Jewish faith. Not just that: he underwent a full-scale transformation, at least externally. He changed his name from the Yiddish "Hirschel" (meaning "deer") to the Protestant "Heinrich" (meaning "estate ruler"). He started attending the local evangelical church, paid tithes, and generally identified as a Christian. From the outside, it looked as if this upstanding man had converted due to a genuine heart change, the classically evangelical "born again" experience. But no such shift had happened.

What had actually occurred in Heinrich's life was this: he got religion to get along. Heinrich believed more in morality than a personal God and reserved his strongest praise for Enlightenment thinkers.[1] Religion for him was less a matter of the soul than a rite of passage into the upwardly mobile European world of free markets and intellectual exchange. As Isaiah Berlin wrote of Heinrich:

> He probably felt no reverence for the Established [Lutheran] Church, but he was even less attached to the Synagogue, and, holding vaguely deist views, saw no moral or social obstacle to complete conformity with the mildly enlightened Lutheranism of his Prussian neighbours.[2]

Inquiring readers may want to know: what prompts all this attention on an obscure lawyer from a small eighteenth-century German town? Because the man in question was named Heinrich Marx, and the son who watched his cynical turn toward utilitarian faith was Karl Marx. Heinrich's nominal religiosity had a profound effect on Karl; he saw his father put on religious airs, and even use religion for gain, but religion was no real phenomenon in and of itself. Small wonder that Marx would later call it "an opiate of the masses," a phrase that has polluted our air ever since and helped to spark one death-filled Marxist "revolution" after another.

The Struggles of Men: Economic Trouble Ahead

Why zero in on all this in a book on the ills of modern men? We start with an aggrieved young Marx because his true story reminds us of disillusionment's great capacity for evil. Disillusionment carries within it the dark arts. It is able to seize upon a wayward soul, manipulate him in secret, and turn him into something malformed. This is true of fake faith, and it is true of our own context—an age that has turned against the order of nature, creating deep confusion and disillusionment in many. This is particularly true of many young men, who show serious signs of tuning out, dropping out, and growing deeply hostile toward their peers and their culture.

This is what is happening all around us today. Few people, however, are paying attention. But we should be—because men are quantifiably struggling in nearly every way possible. As this chapter and the next will reveal, men really do find themselves in a struggle for their very soul, one that affects all dimensions of their existence.

The first area in which we find men struggling is the realm of work. Economically, men are dropping out of the workforce in shocking numbers, as one source shows:

> Male labor force participation rates have been on a steady decline since the 1980s, while women's has been on the rise. In 1960, 93 percent of men aged 25–34 were in the labor force; by 2021, that figure had fallen to 68 percent.[3]

The drop here has been less a measured loss than a tumbling off a cliff. Consider the decrease in workforce participation in just twenty years among sixteen- to twenty-four-year-old men:

> Between 1999 and 2019, the percentage of 16- to 24-year-old males participating in the workforce fell 17 percent and that number is projected to decrease even more over the next 10 years.[4]

As should be apparent, this is a very bad indicator for future societal health. Young men not working equals young men not maturing.

It means those young men are not making a positive contribution to their community and their country. It means they are dropping out at the exact moment that they need to be opting in. It means they are not providing for themselves, and thus that they are not providing for others, which is one of their central callings in life.

Before they can provide for a family, men must be trained to provide for themselves. The picture in America is already bleak. But the trends here hold true elsewhere:

> Other countries, like Italy, France, Spain, Sweden, and Japan, have all seen more than a five-fold increase in young men not employed. The OECD records show that the average unemployment rate for men in their late twenties and early thirties jumped from 2 percent in 1970 to 9 percent in 2012. That is an enormous increase and means millions of young men are not working.[5]

But the narrative gets worse. This book didn't come out in 2019; this book has emerged in the post-lockdown era. The situation is much worse than it was even a half-decade ago. The response to COVID-19 has amplified the trends mentioned above in extremity. Economist Nicholas Eberstadt observes on this count that "average rates of worklessness for prime-age men are...the highest yet for the postwar era."[6] Among working-age men (25 to 54) today, Eberstadt notes, the employment rate is roughly equivalent to that of the Great Depression. This constitutes a "crisis" in his view.[7]

We should not isolate this reality as merely a paycheck problem. Men are made for work, and working for the noble purpose of provision for oneself and others is a huge element of sound manhood. Men who are not working, in short, are men who are almost certainly struggling.

In turn, men who are struggling are men who are volatile, depressed, suicidal, and liable to abandon and even harm their loved ones.

Very few people are paying attention to the work crisis before us. This is both a travesty and a tragedy. The statistics just mentioned taken alone spell disaster not only for men, but for civilization.

Men Are Struggling Educationally

Educationally, we find precisely the same narrative. Men are doing poorly when it comes to school, as college enrollment rates make clear.

> College enrollment has steadily declined following the Great Recession, with total enrollment among both men and women decreasing each year from 2012 to 2020. But many more women than men were enrolling in college when rates began to fall in 2012 (11.6 million women were enrolled at the time, compared to 8.6 million men).[8]

Not every man needs to go to college; indeed, some do well not to do so. But a good number of men should go to college, for they benefit from it, and stand to earn higher wages (on average) than men who do not go to college. At a time when it has never been easier to matriculate and study, however, male student enrollment has plummeted. According to the Brookings Institution,

> Male students now make up a smaller share of all enrolled students in the United States than ever before—just 41 percent of students enrolled in a postsecondary institution in fall 2020 were men.[9]

As mentioned, the post-COVID context has accelerated this trend. No doubt aided and abetted by lockdown policies, college enrollment fell across the board, with some 460,000 students leaving school. But as you would expect—or begin to expect as we continue our doom-read—the enrollment decline reached epic proportions among men. It was *seven times greater* than the disenrollment of women, a truly startling reality. Adrian Huerta, a professor at the University of Southern California, commented on this awful trend with poignant simplicity: "In a sense, we have lost a generation of men to Covid-19." A second professor, Luis Ponjuan of Texas A&M, concurred: "It's a national crisis."[10] An education crisis, yes, but more than that, a manhood crisis.

This is not only happening in the college setting. At every level of education, boys are falling behind girls, and precipitously so. Consider these head-spinning statistics:

> In the U.S, by the eighth grade, only 20 percent of boys are proficient in writing and 24 percent are proficient in reading, versus 41 percent of girls that are proficient in writing and 34 percent that are proficient in reading. Nationally, boys account for 70 percent of all the D's and F's given out at school.[11]

Again, this particular trend is global.

> In some countries like Sweden, Italy, and Poland, girls scored so much higher than boys on reading in the PISA Assessment (a global measure of skills and knowledge) that they were essentially a year to a year and a half ahead in school.[12]

In general terms, a boy and a girl may sit in the same classroom and be part of the same "grade," but the boy is effectively almost two years behind the girl. It is scarcely possible to imagine a worse scenario than the one the data paints. As Ponjuan said, this is a crisis.

Small wonder that studies find boys simply dislike school. In the last forty years, "there has been a 71 percent increase in the number of boys who say they don't like school," according to the Institute for Family Studies.[13] Many boys are failing at school, and boys who are failing are boys who are unmotivated. They will not only face challenges, though; they will leave. According to one source, boys' high school graduation rates are 6 percent lower than females, and in some states, 15 percent lower.[14] Those who stay may well end up diagnosed with ADHD. Boys are given this diagnosis more than twice as often as girls, and part of the reason is because they are placed in contexts that call for sitting, listening, and being quiet.

We should linger on this matter for a moment. Some boys need medication for different conditions, assuredly. But ours is an easily medicated generation. Instead of natural means, people of all kinds receive diagnoses that lead to the prescription—and taking—of powerful drugs. This is true of boys, whose natural energy, assertiveness, and aggressiveness are frequently treated as problems to be cured by medicine and therapy rather than inborn capacities to be stewarded through love and discipline. In truth, boys do often struggle to listen, follow directions, and be quiet. They undoubtedly need discipleship and training in these areas. But in many cases, it is not medication that will address this real challenge effectively; it is shepherding, and the involvement of a loving and disciplined father.

Beyond this, boys need traditional outlets in a serious way. They need to get outside, run around, be creative, burn energy, build things, develop skills, and compete. But our public order allows less and less access to such outlets; in many cases, schools have cut shop class, trade-preparation programs, recess, band, and more. In broad terms, the structure of our public order is not well suited for the welfare and maturation of boys and young men. This demands a multifaceted response, but to return to the matter identified above: wherever possible, let boys be nonmedicated boys.

Men Are Struggling Spiritually

Every man is a sinner by nature. This means that every man since Adam's fall has struggled spiritually. But we need to note as well that men today do have specific spiritual struggles, and we should pay attention to them—because their problems create problems for everyone. This is a many-sided crisis that we will address throughout the text, but at minimum, we can identify two specific spiritual challenges men face in our time.

The first is an addiction to lust, facilitated by pornographic sites and outlets. Men have always struggled with sexual lust, of course, but pornography's increased accessibility has changed the game. About 70 percent of men aged eighteen to twenty-four view pornography on a monthly basis.[15] Here are some additional statistics that should similarly concern us:

- 47 percent of families in the United States report that pornography is a problem in their home.
- Pornography use increases marital infidelity by more than 300 percent.
- 40 percent of people identified as "sex addicts" lose their spouses, 58 percent suffer considerable financial losses, and about 33 percent lose their jobs.

- 68 percent of divorce cases involve one party meeting a new partner over the internet, while 56 percent involve one party having an "obsessive interest" in pornographic websites.[16]

Worldwide, between 50 and 99 percent of men view pornography occasionally, as do 30 to 86 percent of women.[17] Pornography usage is truly a social crisis, and not one that is getting better given the ubiquitous nature of smartphones. Being addicted to it is akin to a disease of the soul—one that eats away at your vitality and steals away your joy in God.

At the same time that many men are losing the battle with temptation, they are not going to church. According to *USA Today*, "Women outnumber men in attendance in every major Christian denomination, and they are 20 percent to 25 percent more likely to attend worship at least weekly."[18] No doubt men have lagged behind women in church attendance in numerous contexts through church history, but we are not presently concerned with history; we are concerned with the fact that in our day, men are not committing to church. This is not a positive reality. It is a very bad situation.

On the other hand, when men do join churches as members, good things happen. By one metric, when a mother comes to Christ, her family will join her at church only 17 percent of the time; but when a father comes to Christ, his family joins him 93 percent of the time.[19] This reminds us of a father's leadership role in the family. If he leads by not going to church, neither joining nor serving it, then it is highly likely that his children will do the same. But if he attends, joins, and serves the church, then his children in many cases follow suit.

Of course, COVID-19 only weakened this situation further, as many churches closed for months and many congregants—both male and female—now consider physical attendance optional. It is very bad for men to have an opt-out choice like this; they need a high standard to meet, and if that does not exist, many will slink away and find excuses for their absence.

Church is essential, and it is essential for producing strong men of God. There is simply no way to raise strong men of Christ without in-person attendance, membership, and service to the local congregation.

Men Are Struggling Physically

In our day, we've witnessed the rise in some circles of what I call Gnostic Manhood. This divorces the soul from the body; it makes spiritual concerns paramount, and essentially divests masculinity of any physical character. A line common to this mindset would sound like, "A true man doesn't care about his grip strength; he cares about getting on his knees in prayer."

It certainly sounds pious, and it does represent an understand-able response to *exaggerated manhood*, which is a real problem. But in truth, Gnostic Manhood is unsound. We cannot separate the soul from the body because we are not souls only. God gave us all the gift of a body, and the body is intimately bound up with our spirituality. This does not mean that physical strength and flourishing is of the greatest importance for men, but neither does it mean that physicality is nothing for men. Paul himself plainly says bodily training "is of some value" (1 Timothy 4:8).

If having a male body is a big part of being a man (as it surely is), then stewarding your body is not a small thing. It's an important element of living as a man to God's glory. In recent years, however, many men have stopped caring about their body, and men as a group have declined physically. One way this manifests is a sharp decrease in grip strength.

> [T]he *Washington Post* highlighted a study showing that the grip strength of a sample of college men had declined significantly between 1985 and 2016. Indeed, the grip strength of the sample of college men had declined so much—from 117 pounds of force to 98—that it now matched that of older Millennial women. In other words, the average college male had no more hand strength than a 30-year-old mom.[20]

This sorry statistic is mirrored by the finding that children take ninety more seconds to run a mile than children did thirty years ago.[21] Running speed is a good test of fitness, and better fitness—contrary to our "body-positive" culture—means lower risk of heart attacks and strokes.[22] According to NPR, this data point represents the culling of fifty studies that included twenty-five million children ages nine to seventeen across the United States, Europe, Australia, New Zealand, and Asia. At a societal level, we are failing our children, for their health is set up to decline and eventually fail.

Men also have demonstrably—and significantly—lower testosterone and sperm counts today. The *Journal of Clinical Endocrinology and Metabolism* found the average sixty-year-old American man in 2004 had testosterone levels 17 percent lower than those of a sixty-year-old in 1987. This study held true among the Danes as well, as researchers reported double-digit declines among men born in the 1960s compared to those born in the 1920s.[23] On the matter of sperm counts, the average male's count has dropped by 62 percent and testosterone rates are down over 30 percent. The largest study on male fertility in history analyzed data from every region on Earth across the last fifty years and found that the average male now has 49 million sperm per milliliter, whereas some fifty years ago, men on average had 104 million sperm per milliliter.[24]

Most of these studies were conducted before the onslaught of global lockdowns in 2020. In a post-COVID world, we may safely assume that the foregoing composite report of men's health has grown only bleaker. Some studies suggest obesity has tripled in developed countries, leading directly to lower testosterone and sperm counts. We can summarize the bleak data given thus far and say this: It is clear beyond a shadow of a doubt that men are struggling physically.

Because the body is tied to the spirit and the soul, when men struggle physically, they are very likely also struggling in other dimensions. The physical affects the spiritual; the spiritual affects the physical. We are not hovering souls, nor are we mere matter. We are *embodied souls*. God has made us a complex mix, and if we embrace Gnostic Manhood, we will surely face real challenges.

Men need to take dominion over their bodies. We must draw on the grace of God and stop making excuses for ourselves. We should reclaim our body as the temple of God (1 Corinthians 6:19). We should not embrace *exaggerated manhood*, but we should receive the body as a gift and steward it well. The Bible does not teach us to embrace self-indulgence, after all. The Bible teaches us to embrace self-rule through the power of the Holy Spirit (Romans 8:1–11). Self-control is a good term, but it's a little weak for what Scripture teaches about how we engage our body. The Apostle Paul wrote that he "beat" his body to bring it under control (1 Corinthians 9:27); you can even translate the Greek word ὑπωπιάζω as "batter," showing us just how intense Paul was regarding his flesh.

Paul's approach to his body was one of ruthless self-discipline empowered by God's grace. He saw that he would either be ruled by his flesh, or his flesh would be ruled by him. He chose the better way, and so should we men today. We should exercise, eat wisely, plan for good sleep as much as we can, get outside often, minimize stress by making wise decisions, and generally fight the weakness of the flesh. We may be struggling physically now, but that need not constitute our death sentence, as it sadly does for many men today.

When discipline takes hold in one area, like our eating, it will inevitably trickle down into other areas. When you start eating well, you're more inclined to exercise. When you start exercising, you're more likely to see other parts of your life that need consistency: reading the Scripture daily, for example, and praying. God has not made us to be disembodied masculine souls; he has made us men, with a male body, and we should honor His design every way we can.

Men Are Struggling Socially

Men, as these findings from the University of Minnesota reveal, commit crime at a disproportionately higher rate than women:

- In 2012, 73.8 percent of all arrestees were males.
- Males accounted for 80.1 percent of people arrested for violent crimes and for 62.6 percent of people arrested for property crimes.
- Males comprised 88.7 percent of people arrested for murder and nonnegligent manslaughter in 2012.
- Of the total number of people arrested for drug abuse violations, 79.7 percent were male.
- Men comprise about 81 percent of all arrests for violent crime and about 63 percent of all arrests for property crime.[25]

To be clear, men have and likely always will commit more aggressive crimes than women. We cannot forget that men are volatile and prone to criminality. Knowing this has proven true over centuries should not make us docile, however; it should instead remind us how high the stakes are with men of every generation.

The very report from which the above data was derived likewise voiced the need to address the problem of male violence—and asked why it exists in the first place, leaning on this telling factoid:

> Some scholars attribute this difference to biological differences between the sexes, but most criminologists attribute it to sociological factors. One of these is gender role socialization: Despite greater recognition of gender roles, we continue to raise our boys to be assertive and aggressive, while we raise our girls to be gentle and nurturing (Lindsey, 2011). Such gender socialization has many effects, and one of these is a large gender difference in criminal behavior.

This is a great example of locking in on a real truth but drawing the wrong conclusion from it. Men are indeed "assertive and aggressive" by nature. But this assertiveness and aggressiveness is not primarily due to "socialization"; these traits are part of the constitution of a boy. He is made for mission. He is built by God for action. You cannot make him otherwise. The only open matter before him is this: will he direct all that natural energy and initiative to good or to ill?

Men Are Struggling in Fatherless Homes

In many cases, boys not only struggle to find help from men, but can barely find one to even ask. A recent piece by Derek Thompson in *The Atlantic* revealed what we know anecdotally: many boys have no male role models.

> This male haphazardness might be reproducing itself among younger generations of men who lack stable role models to point the way to college. Single-parent households have grown significantly more common in the past half century, and 80 percent of those are headed by mothers. This is in part because men are more likely to be incarcerated; more than 90 percent of federal inmates, for example, are men. Men are also less likely to be fixtures of boys' elementary-school experience; about 75 percent of public-school teachers are female. Suggesting that women can't teach boys would be absurd. But the absence of male teachers might be part of a broader absence of men in low-income areas who can model the path to college for boys who are looking for direction.[26]

These statistics hit hard. We should not underplay just how consequential they are. To a startling degree, in different American communities, boys rarely encounter men in their schools; when they return home, there is no man there to shape them. We have heard talk of "food deserts" in recent years; clearly we must also speak of a "man desert." For too many boys today, there are no men to be found.

This is not one moderately troubling problem among many; this is a recipe for certain disaster. It is not too much to say that this is the public crisis of our age. You simply cannot remove boys from the single most important structure of their existence—being raised by a father married to a mother—and think that anything but chaos will follow. Yet this is precisely what is happening in America in our time, and what has been happening for some time. A home without a father is not merely a "single-parent" home (for it is usually men who are gone). Most "single parent" homes are "father absent" homes.

Having a father—even one who is not biologically related—matters so tremendously that it can make all the difference in person's life. According to Thompson's *Atlantic* essay, a 2018 study by the Harvard economist Raj Chetty revealed that

> The few neighborhoods where Black and white boys grew up to have similar adult outcomes were low-poverty areas that also had high levels of "father presence." That is, even boys without a father at home saw significantly more upward mobility when their neighborhood had a large number of fathers present. High-poverty areas without fathers present seem to be doubly impoverished, and boys who live in these neighborhoods are less likely to achieve the milestones, such as college attendance, that lead to a middle-class salary or better.[27]

When we see data like this, we remember that even in the face of sharply divisive claims about the "races," fatherlessness is a universal problem. On the flip side, father presence is a universal solution. It is not an *ultimate* solution, but having fathers present flips the data for boys. It takes them from becoming men who face almost certain jeopardy to those who face a promising tomorrow.

America has gone through a whirlwind devolution of fatherlessness. According to the U.S. Census Bureau, six decades ago, almost 88 percent of children grew up in a home with two married parents. By 2012, that percentage had dropped to 68.[28] That means one of every three children in this country hails from a broken home, regardless of race. According to the Census, "Currently, 55.1 percent of all black children, 31.1 percent of all Hispanic children, and 20.7 percent of all white children are living in single-parent homes."

Children in father-absent homes are almost four times more likely to be poor[29] and abuse drugs and alcohol at "dramatically" greater levels.[30] Children without two parents in the home are significantly more likely to be sexually assaulted, mistreated, and victimized than children with two parents in the home.[31] And saddest of all, children of single-parent homes are more than twice as likely to commit suicide. Children without a father (most often) or mother in the home hit their breaking point far, far more quickly than their peers.

Boys Are Lashing Out

One towering sign that the war on boys is failing horribly is the increase in public shootings over the last few decades, including numerous school shootings. No doubt these terrible events owe to several things—chiefly father absence. Political scientist Warren Farrell has noted this:

> In the 21st century, we know the family backgrounds of six of the seven mass school shooters who killed 10 or more people. In all six, from Salvador Ramos to Adam Lanza, the boys were deprived of their biological father.[32]

Embittered boys without fathers have vented their rage on their peers and their teachers not because our society urges boys to be courageous, but because they come from domestic wreckage—and the lack of a father has wrought terrible effects in their souls.

Seeing this connection should cause every sane person to do everything they can to strengthen men as fathers. As is now clear, a society that targets manhood and downplays the problem of fatherlessness sets itself up for literal death and destruction. It may seem like the jaded loners in our schools are harmless, but as one terrible narrative after another shows, they are not.

There is a horrifying alchemy playing out before us today. Even as our culture voices hostility toward men in many ways (as we shall see below), a bevy of young men react with even greater hostility. They fall through the cracks at some point, but they do not stay there; they come out into public when you least expect it. By then, it is too late—for them and for their victims.

Smash the Patriarchy

It can sound rather strong, one must admit: is there really a "war on men"? Sure, maybe the statistics quoted above show incontrovertibly that men are struggling. But perhaps this is all incidental, an unfortunate but unintended development without any traceable cultural genesis. Couldn't the case I'm building represent an example of "mansplaining"—of being obnoxiously single-minded about a genuinely complex reality? Is it possible that I'm seizing on certain problems, blending them together, and thus concocting a forceful but false narrative out of them?

Some will surely make this case. But I wonder if those who do have listened well to our culture. In a late-feminist age, three of the most common phrases we hear deployed against manhood are these: "Smash the patriarchy," "Masculinity is toxic," and "The future is female."

Let's delve into each of them briefly, understanding their core ideology as best we can. The slogan "smash the patriarchy" starts with a bracing imperative—"smash"—followed by a rather indeterminate target: "the patriarchy." Whatever this problematic force is, we learn very quickly that it deserves the strongest possible action. In truth, "the patriarchy" is simultaneously definite and indefinite. It is something identifiable: the patriarchy. We pick up profoundly sinister vibes here, but where the headquarters of this movement are found, we do not know.

An article on the Cambridge University website gives some clarity, if not much. Feminism, says one young woman, "should not only be about identity, but how identity is linked to oppressive structures."[33] What are these structures? Some listed include "austerity, racist policing, borders, prisons and other issues." Later in the article, the following social ills draw fire: "the Trump presidency" alongside "the rise of far-right groups seeking to restrict women's reproductive rights and actively propagate misogynistic attitudes." These factors give way to a call to "show solidarity with women experiencing violence or oppression" as one young feminist publisher puts it.[34]

According to this article, modern feminism seeks to take down "oppressive structures." This is a classically Marxist idea. Ostensibly, any sane person opposes oppression, but the young feminists quoted in this rather strange piece seem to find oppression anywhere there is an authoritative limit or boundary. Borders are bad; prisons are bad; controlled spending is bad; restricting abortion is bad. These institutions can suffer corruption, sure, but it is foolish to claim that national borders—as just one example—are inherently oppressive.

In reality, in formulations like these, the neutral is blended with the obviously bad to create a boogeyman—"the patriarchy"—that must be attacked. The plight of women who are assaulted (a terrible evil) is conflated with the existence of prisons. The two realities, it is argued, reveal systemic oppression, when in reality there is no such correlation. Smashing the patriarchy ends up meaning, for the most part, opposing even mild conservatism, the kind that supports national borders and penitentiaries and the right to life.

Conceived this way, "smash the patriarchy" ends up meaning "smash conservatism." A recent ACLU event in Oklahoma reflected just such an instinct, as its description made clear: "Roundtable discussions full of fear and uncertainty, rallies that publicize peoples' personal stories, the continued criminalization of pregnant people and providers, the lack of access to healthcare, THE PATRIARCHY; it's all too much." Those feeling such depths of emotion were encouraged to assemble for an angry healing session: "Join as we write and talk about our feelings about abortion bans, share space with like-minded people, SMASH something, and most importantly let's do it all in a safe space. See you there!"[35]

In vitriol like this, the patriarchy is less a tangible body of enemies and more a generic malevolence transmitted by men. For reasons that are not spelled out here (as is often the case), men are the problem in this equation. Men get women pregnant against their will; men then criminalize abortion (called "healthcare" here); and men leave women in a state of unresolvable but fully justified rage. Men are everywhere bad, everywhere guilty, and must thus be targeted and, well, "smashed."

Men Are Toxic

The above campaign presents a generalized view of men. But "Smash the patriarchy" is not the only slogan that does so. As we covered at some length in the Introduction, the phrase "toxic masculinity" has become ubiquitous in our culture and is not accompanied by an equivalent label regarding womanhood like "toxic femininity." No, "toxic masculinity" stands alone, and it has seared itself onto the public consciousness. "Toxic masculinity" is a short phrase that captures a much bigger outlook: men are toxic. Manhood, at least traditional manhood, is deeply problematic. As such, it must be unlearned and undone.

But here again inquiring minds cannot help but ask: What exactly is "toxic masculinity"? If it is the great evil it is said to be, surely we need some skin on these bones? A Brown University website purports to give some definition. Under the auspices of social wellbeing, Brown gives this guidance on a page titled "Unlearning Toxic Masculinity":

> Rigid definitions of masculinity are toxic to men's health. Even the World Health Organization (WHO) has recognized that men's tendency to die at younger ages may correlate to the harmful ways that masculinity has been defined in society and the ways that men have been conditioned to practice it.[36]

According to this article, "risk-taking behaviors and lack of willingness to seek help were among the reasons for negative health outcomes" experienced by men.[37]

We know that men do indeed live unwisely and sinfully. We will explore this in later chapters, rooting this tendency in theological truth rather than mere social conditioning. Men who prey on others deserve strenuous rebuke and serious consequences, and the Bible has much to say about this subject. Further, men need education in wise living and should seek help as they need it (and we all need it). But leftist outlets like Brown University mix in severely problematic claims as they identify real weaknesses of men. "Risk-taking behaviors" can be bad, but they also can be good. The man who runs into a burning building to save a helpless baby is taking a risk, and doing so virtuously. The man who starts a company to provide for his family after much planning and preparation is taking a risk, and a good one at that. Risk-taking is not an inherent evil, though this website—echoing much common thinking of our time—presents it as such.

Yet this is not the biggest problem before us. The site straightforwardly affirms that "rigid definitions of masculinity are toxic to men's health." This is linguistic sleight of hand; "rigid" basically means "stable." In the simplest terms, Brown University is peddling nonsense here. It presents biblical manhood, for example, as a "toxic" threat, when in truth men need to learn biblical manhood desperately. Almost nothing is crueler than leaving men without an understanding of what it means to be a man and robbing them of a followable script. Yet this is the first move that woke leftism makes. It presents traditional manhood as "toxic" without any substantiation or proof, and it offers up fluid and "unrigid" manhood as the solution. Is it any wonder that many young men today have no idea what it means to be a man?

Other sources concur with Brown's toxic counsel. One British website, Aurora, offers the following as proof of "toxic masculinity": not "displaying emotion"; not being a "feminist ally"; and again, "risk-taking."[38] Men, it should be noted, should show some emotion. But men also must control and discipline their emotions. This is especially pertinent because male emotions can run strong in certain areas, meaning boys must be trained to endure and bear up amidst hardship.

Further, men should protect women, but it is in no way true that failing to support "feminist activism" constitutes unsound behavior. Lastly, as we have observed, men can foolishly take risks, but they also can put their innate bent for risk to good use, provided they pursue virtuous ends by virtuous means. Yet here is the lens by which numerous voices today justify their despisal of men. Men are "toxic," and those who are toxic must be reconditioned, reprogrammed, and—if they will not give up traditional notions of manhood—destroyed.

An army of leftist advocates has arisen to execute this very task. Therapists help to reengineer the "toxic masculine" worldview;

classrooms aid in the reeducation of boys drawn to strong manhood; doctors prescribe heavy medication to tamp down the natural aggression and adventurousness of young men who persist in being boyish; gender experts lead the charge publicly on men who still dare to act like men. Even if many traditional men seek to lead productive lives in natural terms, when men do commit real crimes, leftist journalists will work with skill and swiftness to tie the wayward outliers to the broader group.

The Church will say little in response—and ordinary men will languish, struggle, lash out, and drop out.

The Future Is Female

In the fallout of her failed presidential run, Hillary Clinton trotted out one of the classic feminist maxims: "Despite all the challenges we face," Clinton said, "I remain convinced that yes, the future is female." Having cited Clinton, *The Washington Post* indulged a moment of nostalgia for recent days gone by: "'The future is female' is a phrase that was invoked often by Clinton's supporters during her campaign for president and in recent years has become a rallying cry among women and feminists who advocate for more female everything."[39] Not just a rallying cry, it turns out; according to the *Post*, enterprising feminists are making good money off this phrase (and others). Anticapitalism, we see, can be good business.

Clinton deployed the slogan to transmit the inevitability of her female presidency. She was the one history was waiting for, but in a massive upsurge of what some would call "the Patriarchy," Clinton lost the election to Donald Trump. This disruptive event notwithstanding, the slogan endures. For example, a singer who goes by the name of Madame Gandhi wrote this to exposit "the future is female":

The future is female does not mean female over male, nor is it trans-misogynist. The future is female means that we will no longer live in a world that believes that hierarchy and zero sum games are the only viable forms of social organization. It instead offers up the alternative that each person has something unique to contribute to the world, and therefore our job as an interconnected [species] is to create space for each person to be their best and most authentic self so that they can contribute their gift. The slogan suggests that circular organizations of leadership may serve each of us better than hierarchical ones.[40]

The identifiable elements of the old, bad male order seem to Madame Gandhi to be "hierarchy" and competition. Hierarchical structures, of course, can suffer abuse, but so can "circular" structures. The corruption of human nature diffuses across all forms of social organization; sin is no respecter of org charts. Even the voicing of this view in public suggests that Madame Gandhi is some kind of leader, reminding us that it is easier to critique the old ways of leadership than to truly supplant them.

A female future supposedly does away with harmful competition. But in truth, competition actually makes way for people to "contribute their gift." Is it true that men can compete in sometimes unneeded and even ridiculous ways? Yes, it is. But "the future is female" slogan undervalues what men bring to the table, and intentionally so. After all, according to Madame Gandhi, we live in the age of "female energy." According to her, this means that "we live in a world that is emotionally intelligent. A world that is collaborative. A world in which we are linked and not ranked, as Gloria Steinem has brilliantly explained."[41] This may sound fine, but rather indefinite. How do you run a business in a cutthroat market in a "collaborative" way? When five competitors wish to overtake your spot on the charts, what does being "emotionally intelligent" get you?

Weirdly, the "female future" itself is undergoing renovation. Now, the future is "fluid." Tegan and Sara, a Canadian musical duo, made this point in a voiceover:

> The future is relationships that look different
> Families that look different
> A world so different—none of it is considered different anymore
> The future is not believing all the ways they've told you— you aren't enough
> You ARE enough. You are the future.[42]

This is actually where the feminist movement stands: it's in complete disorder. The "female future" no longer looks so bright and promising; the "genderfluid" movement of our day disdains the pantsuit power feminism of past decades. To be clear, feminism of our day is markedly anti-man and pro-woman. But womanhood no longer has an essential character. Womanhood is not one thing; it's whatever you want it to be. "Different" is in; stability is out. If this ends up meaning that a six foot four, three hundred-pound man wants to identify as a woman and use the ladies' restroom, then he is right to do so. He is "enough," one can conclude. In a genderfluid age, he is the future.

Conclusion

The future is a key focus of the enemies of men. The stakes are high in this game. Though woke feminism scorches the masculine penchant for risk-taking, this same movement is taking a considerable risk indeed. It dares to dream of a future that is not male and that, in fact, has precious little place for men in days ahead. But this is a future that is no future at all. The social reengineering burden assumed by our post-male world is too great for us. Men cannot be made to be anything but men.

Thankfully, we are not left with only this foul and foolish ideology. Later in this book, we will see a better way forward for men—one that does not involve their obsolescence, but rather their remaking in Christ.

But before we get to the hope that every man (and every person) has in the Word and the Gospel, we need to think more about what has led us to our present fractured state. Having thus far shown that men are struggling, and having addressed some of the messages that boys and men are hearing, we now dig deeper still. We look not simply at *how* men are struggling, but *why*. The war is on—but we must see who is waging it, and with what ideological weaponry.

CHAPTER 2

Why Men Are Struggling

We laugh at honor and are shocked to find
traitors in our midst.

C. S. Lewis

It was early May 2022, and I had just flown across the country, arriving in Washington, D.C. When I stepped off the plane about 10:00 p.m. eastern time, my phone immediately started buzzing. Trying to hail a cab, I ignored the texts coming in until one caught my eye: "Did you see the news about SCOTUS?" That stopped me in my tracks. Word was that *Roe v. Wade* was going to be overturned. Suffice to say that it was difficult to sleep that night.

The next evening, a friend and I headed over to the Supreme Court. There were scores of protestors outside, a mob unlike anything I have ever seen. The rage was thick; the venom was everywhere; many of the protestors were nearly unhinged. They "shouted their abortion." They chanted against conservative justices. They solemnly stood together in a line holding signs that spelled "BANS OFF OUR BODIES." The entire experience was a curious blend of the bellicose, the tribal, and the worshipful.

The moment that etched itself in my memory came next: I wandered over to a loose semicircle of chanters. Someone had brought out a portable speaker, and various pro-abortion women spoke up—usually with great vulgarity—about their right to kill babies. Then a man took the mic to lead the crowd in a series of chants. The most unexpected was this: "ALL MEN LIE!" he fairly screamed. The crowd followed him. Here was irony of the richest sort: a man savaging men, saying that all men lie—and no one realizing that if this idea held true, he was lying at that very moment. The hypocrisy of that chant may have been lost on many, but its message was not. They instinctually responded to it, blaming and indicting men for vague and unsubstantiated crimes. Truly, this is one of the most dependable rallying points in our culture today: assail men, and you're sure both to draw a crowd and get heads nodding in agreement.

Ironically, all sides agree on one point: we are troubled as a society over men. Further, anyone who is willing to be objective can see that men are genuinely and quantifiably in danger today, and boys are in even worse peril. But *why* are boys struggling? Why are men disappearing, going soft, exaggerating themselves, or embracing evil?

Why Men Are Struggling: 7 Key Factors

Amidst other factors we could identify, we will consider several specific contributors to this sorry situation. Knowing these seven cultural, social, and intellectual trends will help us make sense of where we are—and that, in turn, will help us know how to address the travails of men with the Word, the Gospel, and the truth.

Factor #1: The Philosophical Assault on the Family
We have already considered a slice of Marx's story. On the strength of his spiritually troubling boyhood, Marx grew up to become one

of history's most consequential leaders, and not for the good. In *The Communist Manifesto*, Marx and his cowriter Friedrich Engels called for a gentle social reform program that began with this mild-mannered assertion: "Abolition of the family!"

This isn't a wild-eyed take on Marx and Engels. As so often is the case, they stated their ambitions far more zealously than many historians have. Read their words for yourself:

> On what foundation is the present family, the bourgeois family, based? On capital, on private gain. In its completely developed form, this family exists only among the bourgeoisie. But this state of things finds its complement in the practical absence of the family among the proletarians, and in public prostitution. The bourgeois family will vanish as a matter of course when its complement vanishes, and both will vanish with the vanishing of capital. Do you charge us with wanting to stop the exploitation of children by their parents? To this crime we plead guilty. But, you say, we destroy the most hallowed of relations, when we replace home education by social.[1]

We must not fail to note just how radical this paragraph is. Because the free market—unkindly called "capitalism" here—is evil in their view, the family structure that accords with freedom is evil as well. For Marx and Engels, most anything private and sacred is bad. Private property is bad, private wealth is bad, and relatedly, individual liberty is bad. Add to this list the very significant institution of the family, the private center of life: It must not only go through some change for Marx and Engels; it must "vanish."

This anti-program will supposedly stop child "exploitation." In truth, Marx's evil scheme has led and will lead to untold human suffering as children lose the structure God ordered for their good: a father and a mother. Whatever schooling decision parents make, "home education" must take place as Dad and Mom raise their kids to know truth, goodness, and beauty. But Marx wanted such training ended, and so have a chorus of others over the last century.

Many decades later, in the mid-twentieth century, the Marxist Frankfurt School and others launched their own campaign to destroy the family, which they viewed through the prism of repression. In this scheme, their basic line was this: the individual must be free, completely free, to do whatever they like. Any and all institutions that oppose this vision are evil and should be overcome. As one would likely suspect, this meant the natural family fostered repression. Fathers stood at the forefront of the family, and so represented the key figure to take down. So said cultural critic Philip Rieff:

> The chief institutional instrument of repressive authority is the family. As a political revolution must overthrow the power of the state, moral revolution must overthrow the power of the family—all families.... A revolution must sweep out the family and its ruler, the father, no less cleanly than the old political gangs and their leaders. However radical the revolution, so long as the family persists, authority will creep back.[2]

Wherever attacks on the natural family appear, assaults on fatherhood follow. In fact, fatherhood is the central target of such attempts to destroy God-created order. If the father is the head of the natural family, then all one needs to do to topple that structure is undermine and ultimately remove fathers from their role as authority figures In the home. It is like pushing the single domino that knocks down the whole stack.

Today, leftists in various countries agitate for total social control of children, the fulfillment of Marx's dark vision. In recent years, the organization called Black Lives Matter has championed a radical and transgressive family policy. After being criticized for its openly anti-family stance, BLM erased from its website what you will now read. Calling their work "a radical social intervention," they swore themselves and their followers to these commitments:

> We disrupt the Western-prescribed nuclear family structure requirement by supporting each other as extended families and "villages" that collectively care for one another, especially "our" children, to the degree that mothers, parents, and children are comfortable.[3]

BLM is simply repristinating Marx's foul precepts, seeking to "dismantle" the creation order that God has made. Further, as you probably noted, BLM's radical statement writes fathers out of the picture entirely. Men apparently have no place in the sprawling villages of BLM's utopia. At least, they are not named. Of course, we cannot help but point out that even if men have no explicit place in the disrupted world of BLM, boys would still be born to the disrupters following this movement. One wonders what will be done to those boys as they grow up.

The family is and has been under philosophical assault in the West for many decades now. Men as the heads of homes have taken the most ferocious portion of this broadside. Small wonder that many men are struggling and have little or no inclination or clue how to lead a family.

Factor #2: The Ascendancy and Dominance of Feminism

We now live in a feminist society, so like the frog in the kettle, we may not even be aware how hot it's become. But suffice to say that we have transitioned out of a public order driven by men and masculine prerogatives, and into one driven by women and feminine prerogatives.

This transition is easily documentable due to the march of the various "waves" of feminism. First-wave feminism of the Gilded Age sought equal public rights for women; second-wave feminism focused on the abolition of traditional gender constraints so that women would be able to do whatever men did; and third-wave feminism pushed "reproductive rights" and the liberation of women from all perceived forms of oppression. Of late, fourth-wave feminism has somewhat ironically embraced post-gender visions of womanhood, plunging the entire feminist movement into disarray.

Tracing the history of feminism is a task larger than we can undertake here. However, we can chart how feminists have attacked manhood over the years, thus succeeding in both demeaning masculinity and reworking womanhood. As we shall see, these attacks have not only affected the cultural conception of manhood but have led to ironic and unexpected consequences for women as well.

Writing in the postwar years, the French feminist Simone de Beauvoir pictured the traditional feminine domesticity as a kind of prison sentence. She painted the female homemaker as bound to a system of "slavery" and sought to convince her readers of the utter grimness of this system:

Few tasks are more like the torture of Sisyphus than housework, with its endless repetition: the clean becomes soiled, the soiled is made clean, over and over, day after day. The housewife wears herself out marking time: she makes nothing, simply perpetuates the present . . . Eating, sleeping, cleaning—the years no longer rise up towards heaven, they lie spread out ahead, grey and identical. The battle against dust and dirt is never won.[4]

In the view of de Beauvoir and her peers, the domestic vocation was effectively injurious to women. God did not call them to such a role, nor did it bear glory within it. Those who advocated for men to be providers and women to be homemakers instead trapped women in a bleak and bitter life that in truth was not really worth living. Feminism thus took on the brand of a liberating force, freeing women from the shackles of rearing children and cultivating the home. The traditional "division of labor" did not owe to any inherent wiring or creational intent. Patriarchy dominated the world and subjugated women.

As feminists came of age, they trained their sights on the very makeup of the family itself. Branding the natural or biblical family the "nuclear family," they called for its obliteration. Linda Gordon, a longtime academic, famously said, "The nuclear family must be destroyed.... Whatever its ultimate meaning, the breakup of families now is an objectively revolutionary process."[5] *Ms.* magazine editor Robin Morgan concurred, zeroing in on marriage as the means by which the trap closed shut on women: "We can't destroy the inequities between men and women until we destroy marriage."[6] Outspoken activists Nancy Lehmann and Helen Sullinger charged in similar terms that feminists needed to "work to destroy" the institution of marriage, for doing so was "a necessary condition for the liberation of women. Therefore it is important for us to encourage women to leave their husbands and not to live individually with men."[7]

Nor did feminists stop with targeting marriage and traditional womanhood. They went after men themselves. Morgan famously said this:

I feel that "man-hating" is an honorable and viable political act, that the oppressed have a right to class-hatred against the class that is oppressing them.[8]

Perhaps the most virulent of the feminists, Andrea Dworkin, framed sex as a violent "occupation" of women. She saw men as the wrongful aggressor against women in all sexual encounters, for

[i]n the experience of intercourse, she loses the Capacity for integrity because her body—the basis of privacy and freedom in the material world for all human beings—is entered and occupied; the boundaries of her physical body are—neutrally speaking—violated.[9]

Sadly, Dworkin seemed unable to trust men at all, so jaded was her view: "Under patriarchy, every woman's son is her potential betrayer and also the inevitable rapist or exploiter of another woman."[10] This meant to some feminists that men needed not simply to step back, but to die out, as Boston College professor Mary Daly put it none too gently:

If life is to survive on this planet, there must be a decontamination of the earth. I think this will be accompanied by an evolutionary process that will result in a drastic reduction of the population of males.[11]

Feminism underwent further evolution as the twentieth century drew to a close. Having successfully convinced many that traditional female roles were inherently oppressive, the feminists came to question the very idea of womanhood itself. One of the leading authorities in this effort was Judith Butler, a professor of gender studies at the University of California-Berkeley. Butler made an argument that initially sounded exotic but now has many adherents:

> Significantly, if gender is instituted through acts which are internally discontinuous, then the appearance of substance is precisely that, a constructed identity, a performative accomplishment which the mundane social audience, including the actors themselves, come to believe and to perform in the mode of belief.[12]

Butler proved to be a key voice in shifting discussion surrounding manhood and womanhood away from sex—something biological and fixed—to gender, which is "constructed" and performative.

This is a very important argument. It has been extremely influential over the last twenty years of American cultural and public life. In Butler's handling, one acts out one's innate gender in a drama-like performance, but such real-life thespianism does not owe to any concrete notion of manhood, womanhood, or any other identity. According to Butler, if gender is merely performative, then there is "no true or false, real or distorted acts of gender, and the postulation of a true gender identity would be revealed as a regulatory fiction."[13] So "the very notions of an essential sex, a true or abiding masculinity or femininity, are also constituted as part of the strategy by which the performative aspect of gender is concealed."[14]

The takeaway is plain: There is no such thing as manhood (or womanhood). There is only performance. To update Shakespeare, all the world's a stage, and every person is an actor in their own off-Broadway gender drama. Children do not know that they are in such a context, but there are adults all around them who long to shape them in their foul image. So said C. S. Lewis many years ago:

The difference between the old and the new education will be an important one. Where the old initiated, the new merely "conditions." The old dealt with its pupils as grown birds deal with young birds when they teach them to fly; the new deals with them more as the poultry-keeper deals with young birds—making them thus or thus for purposes of which the birds know nothing. In a word, the old was a kind of propagation —men transmitting manhood to men; the new is merely propaganda.[15]

So much for *auld lang syne*: "men transmitting manhood to man." Amazing as it sounds, schools used to exist to help accomplish just such an aim. Those days are gone like shadow on the mountain. What Lewis would have made of our day and its noxious "propaganda," we can only imagine.

If all the foregoing seems like a strange rainbow-punch-mix of ideas, it's because it is. We simultaneously live now in a deeply feminist public order, but also a profoundly anti-feminist public order. What do I mean? As I surfaced in Chapter 1, womanhood is now recognized as the dominant sex in many contexts, or at least treated as if it should be. Women set the tone, and women—many believe—*should* set the tone. Not for nothing did Kay Hymowitz label the era in question—roughly the last thirty years of the twentieth century— "the new Girl Order." Girls dominated pop culture, dominated the academy, and in many cases, dominated men.[16]

But at the same time, we are told without any irony that there is no such thing as womanhood in any fixed sense. In the eyes of Butler and her ilk, there is only "performed" gender. I do not exaggerate when I say that we could not find ourselves in greater chaos than we presently do. The future is female, we hear one minute, but the next we hear that there is no such thing as male or female—there is only your own self-perceived gender. A more confusing and contradictory cocktail of worldviews you can scarcely find.

This hypocrisy is especially troubling because it has gone medical. Children who experience "gender dysphoria" are now regularly encouraged to get body-warping surgery at very young ages to fit their "gender identity." Deborah Soh rightly identifies how wrong this is: "Physicians won't even allow adult women to make a decision about tying their tubes or having a hysterectomy until they are in their thirties" and yet these same doctors "argue that an eight-year-old has the emotional maturity to begin the medical process of identifying as the opposite sex."[17] Children are in danger today—grave danger. Very few people, however, dare to say so, and when they do, they pay a steep price.

The ideologies sketched above have had very bad effects on kids in general. Leaving aside the dangers of normalizing "transgender" identity and gender "transitions," we can see how boys have been impacted by feminism in major ways. Here is just one example: As we have alluded to, the traits of boys are frequently presented as "antisocial" (and negative), while the traits of girls are frequently presented as "social" (and positive).

This might sound fine, but it really is anything but fine. The terms are a tell: Traditionally masculine traits like risk-taking, aggressiveness, adventure-seeking, boldness, and declarative speech are portrayed as harmful to others, while traditionally feminine traits like listening, collaborating, seeking out other viewpoints, and empathy are portrayed as healing to others. For this reason, many argue, our society should transition out of a masculine mold into a feminine one. Gone are the days of angry male CEOs in the business world, for example; in are the days of compassionate female CEOs who seek the good of all, not just their own company.

Society has shifted accordingly. Increasingly, our institutions are not structured for freedom, exploration, challenges, risk, and the development of bold character. Frequently, they are structured to develop groupthink, to minimize risk, and develop conformist character. In noting this, I do not imply that everything traditionally masculine is good, nor that everything traditionally feminine is bad. To the contrary, God filled the earth with both men and women, and thus there is great good in both manhood and womanhood.

But for our purposes, we cannot miss this: It is a very bad idea to read what is masculine as deficient and harmful. This is exactly the idea that lies behind much criticism of manhood and men today; as this book attempts, we must find a way to urge men upward while never committing the tragic error of reading manhood as inherently worse than womanhood. No such conclusion follows from sound biblical thinking, as we shall explore below. We are urged today to see masculinity as bad, but we must reject this view. Said more spiritually, we must think according to Scripture, not culture.

We return to our discussion of the state of our public order. The push for a kinder and gentler world came at the same time as the call for women to "lean in." Sheryl Sandberg, the business executive who coined this phrase, may not have directly told men to "lean back," but that was the generally unstated idea. In these terms, twenty-first-century feminists have effectively declared the age of men to be over. For example, Hanna Rosin trumpeted nothing less than "the end of men" in her much-applauded 2013 book by that title. The central good of Rosin's program seems to have been women advancing by their own self-chosen path. This commitment led her, shockingly, to champion "hook-up culture" as a means for female growth and self-discovery:

Zoom out and you see that for most women the hook-up culture is like an island they visit mostly during their college years, and even then only when they are bored or experimenting or don't know any better. But it is not a place where they drown. The sexual culture may be more coarse these days, but young women are more than adequately equipped to handle it, because unlike in earlier ages they have more important things going on, such as good grades and internships and job interviews and a financial future of their own to worry about.[18]

Rosin concluded this strange tangent by an appeal to data:

> The most patient and thorough research about the hook-up culture shows that over the long run, women benefit greatly from living in a world where they can have sexual adventure without commitment or all that much shame, and where they can enter into temporary relationships that don't derail their careers.[19]

What a revision of the old sexual order this represents. Instead of men protecting women and pursuing one woman as their wife, Rosin reads collegiate hook-up culture as a proving ground for ambitious young women. Covenant sexuality of a historic Christian kind is out; "sexual adventure" is in. As Rosin sees it, young women do well to explore their sexual interests for a season, knowing all the while that they need not fail to lay hold of the great goal of many twentieth-century feminists or "derail their careers."

What a shallow and malformed vision of womanhood this is. What a bad system for both men and women "hook-up culture" represents. It does indeed train young women to be adventurous, but such sexual tourism is good for neither men nor women. This kind of system trains young people to use one another sexually, not love and cherish each other in lifelong union. Gone is chivalry. Men, in fact, should just chill out and embrace the new paradigm. Rosin urges men to "stop looking back, fretting that all the 'real men' are dead, and allow themselves to go soft, a little."[20] Here is an explicit call for "soft men."

We can make a similar point with the #MeToo era. The sexual revolution undoubtedly encouraged men to act like animals—and many did, to their shame and dissolution, as did many women. The real abuses catalogued under #MeToo that were committed by men deserve the full justice of our legal system. We cannot help but note, however, that in the hands of some, #MeToo represented more than just a quest for justice on the part of some genuinely wronged women; it also was used to hunt down and destroy men, and to advance the argument that manhood is inherently wicked and predatory.

For some, this movement seemed to be a kind of open vendetta, with any man accused being seen as essentially guilty until proven innocent—and perhaps not even then. Such an assumption is often based on Marxist power dynamics, a system that places blame and guilt on those who have power. This leaves those not in power as automatic victims, essentially.

There is much to say about this phenomenon. Men in power really do sin, and should be held to account when they do. Christians, of all people, most want justice when sin occurs, and as moral realists, we know that sin is a scourge in our world. However, our adjudication of accusations must not depend on the Marxist power dynamics of Critical Theory. Nor can we embrace a naïve, Pollyannaish view of the world, where women never commit sin and never hold any responsibility in given encounters. Each case must be judged on its own merits. But we must take care that we do not predetermine anyone's fate.

While the movement in question eventually lost steam, it had a real effect on our culture, as has the feminist movement writ large. Boys get sent to the confession booths, girls don't. Men are called out by pastors for their sins, while women get only praise. Businesses get rewarded for being "women-run companies," with no concurrent benefits for men-run outfits. These trends and others like them reflect a feminist public order.

In this order, women are set up to thrive, and men are not; women are encouraged to lead, and men are urged to step back. Though this system is sold to us in glowing terms, it is in truth a net positive for no one because it goes against God-created nature and teaching.

Factor #3: The Theological Attack on the Fatherhood of God and Order of Leadership

Many Christians have been raised to adore God the Father. When this is discussed in detail, a responsible Bible teacher will communicate that God the Father does not have a physical body, of course; God is spirit, not corporeal. Nonetheless, the Father has an exclusively masculine identity throughout the Bible, and Scripture directs us to address the first person of the Godhead not as Mother, but as Father. The name "Father," then, is not a give-or-take title that can be swapped out according to the whims of culture. God the Father stands at the head of the Christian faith, and He adopts us as His own children through the blood of His Son and the regeneration of the Spirit.

It will not likely surprise you that the aforementioned feminist movement took hard aim at this vital truth. The religious wing of feminism was, if anything, even more militant than the secular wing. Mary Daly, for example, famously said that "if God is male, then male is God."[21] She reconceived God not as Father, but as "the ultimate Final Cause," the one named "She Who Attracts." What does this mean, exactly? For her, it meant that God is

the constantly Unfolding Verb of Verbs who is intransitive, who has no object that limits her dynamism. She is

the Good who is Self-communicating, who is the Verb
from whom, in whom, and with whom all true movements
move. That is, She is, of course, Be-ing.[22]

I confess as a theologian that I have no idea what any of this
means. Not to be outdone, fellow feminist professor Rosemary
Radford Ruether characterized God in similar terms, celebrating
"God's Shekinah, Holy Wisdom, the Mother-face of God has fled
from the high thrones of patriarchy and has gone into exodus with
us."[23]

In truth, the feminist movement had long cultivated an attack
on God the Father. If one could erase God's male identity, then one
could displace strong manhood from Christianity. If one succeeded in
this grand aim, one would largely remove strong manhood from the
Church. If one succeeded there, one would vanquish strong manhood
in society. This is what "death of God" theologian William Hamilton
wrote in celebration of his own ideology:

The death of God in 1965 made the feminist theology of
the 1970s possible as ideology, if not convincing as theology, because it removed the masculine-aggressive principle from the Christian drama of redemption.[24]

This is a telling admission on the part of an avowed despiser
of biblical manhood, biblical Christianity, and the biblical Christ.
The feminist theologians, like the "death of God" theologians of
the 1960s, positively despise the "masculine-aggressive principle"
of the Gospel. God, in truth, is their ultimate target. Those that still
confess belief in God the Father removed any concept of authority
and leadership from Him. The Father is just a proper name, nothing
more; the Father was stripped of any leadership capacity. What these

theologians did to the Divine Person, they would surely do to human fathers.

The attacks did not stop there. As we have seen, some in the feminist movement sought to change the very identity of God the Father to that of God the Mother. Here is audacity that would make a demon blush: changing the given name and identity of Almighty God. At the congregational and domestic level, feminists argued vehemently against men being the elders of the Church and heads of the home; in time, evangelical "egalitarians" proposed exegetical and theological cases for women becoming elders, and "headship" in the home being shared by husband and wife alike, as the spouses practiced "mutual submission."

They did not stop there and have not stopped in our time. The feminist theologians changed nothing less than the Lord's Prayer, which famously reads as follows:

> Our Father in heaven,
> hallowed be your name.
> Your kingdom come,
> your will be done,
> on earth as it is in heaven.
> Give us this day our daily bread,
> and forgive us our debts,
> as we also have forgiven our debtors.
> And lead us not into temptation,
> but deliver us from evil. (Matthew 6:9–13)

The Lord's Prayer, we note, is the "model prayer" that Christ gave in response to His disciples asking Him to teach them how to pray. Christ did not direct their prayer to Himself or to the Spirit, but rather led His followers to pray to God the Father. The feminist theologians of recent days, however, have revised Christ's prayer.[25]

They have produced the following revision—entitled "Our Mother Who Is within Us"—to overcome the inherent patriarchy apparently built into Christ's mind:

> Our Mother who is within us
> we celebrate your many names.
> Your wisdom come.
> Your will be done,
> unfolding from the depths within us.
> Each day you give us all that we need.
> You remind us of our limits
> and we let go.
> You support us in our power
> and we act with courage.
> For you are the dwelling place within us
> the empowerment around us
> and the celebration among us
> now and forever. Amen.[26]

Feminist liturgy does not stop with the above-quoted blasphemy. A self-professed "goddess feminist" penned the following short paean to the Goddess:

> Hail Goddess full of grace. Blessed are you and blessed are
> all the fruits of your womb. For you are the MOTHER of
> us all. Hear us now and in all our needs. O blessed be, O
> blessed be. Amen.[27]

All the above pressure had had a major effect on the Christian Church. In some circles, simply praying to God the Father is now considered toxic and patriarchal; doing so is offensive to women, as it excludes femininity from the divine identity. The aforementioned efforts to change divine identity have had many effects on many churches, causing them to see the Fatherhood of God as problematic, opening the door for a feminist and egalitarian spirit to enter the Church. Women and men share leadership in the home and church, compromising the order of creation and design of God. The Church increasingly looks more and more like the world—which is just what the feminist theologians wanted.

Factor #4: Replacing Defined Manhood with Androgyny

Once you see "the Genderbread Person," you can never unsee it. I'm not sure when I had the misfortune to first see this image, but I cannot forget it. Instead of the gingerbread man, which I vaguely recall from childhood, various institutions in our culture now champion the genderfluid person. According to the creator of "the Genderbread Person," you can have a male or female "biological sex" (your anatomy) but have a different "gender identity" (what gender you perceive yourself to be), as well as your own unique "gender expression" (how you "demonstrate" your gender).[28]

The harvest of deconstruction that we have already discussed in this chapter has led us to this moment in history: like this strange fictitious creature, we are now an exercise in self-perception. Our lived reality involves creating our outward self, based on our internal understanding of who we truly are. We may have a male body but a female gender identity, or vice versa. If this is the case, we will present ourselves in a female way—but even there, we may blur the lines a good bit. It is not unusual in 2023 to see a person who is biologically male dressing in women's clothes while also having stubble on his face and a shaved head. Even more than strictly conforming to an opposite-sex presentation, androgyny is in. Fluidity is the rule. Transgender is the leading edge of culture.

In this new age, gender-bending is not the exception, but the rule. Eli Erlick, director of the decade-old organization Trans Student Educational Resources, said:

> If someone imagines a future where womanhood and femaleness are accessible and collectively working toward justice, then that is perfectly fine. Gender is not the problem, gender roles are. Fluid identities—queerness, gender fluidity, gender nonconformity, etc.—are not more subversive than "female," and all marginalized communities are the future.[29]

Fluidity, then, is the new stability. Nonconformity is the new standard. The gender binary is out; the nonbinary rules the roost, separating the good from the bad. If there is real irony coursing through this new ideology, there is also real militancy. The new gender order is no less insistent that it is right (and all competitors are wrong) than the old one.

Earlier, we referenced Black Lives Matter positioning itself as the voice of intersectional justice. On the sexual front, BLM's now-erased statement expressed a desire to liberate society from binary categories:

> We are committed to fostering a queer-affirming network. When we gather, we do so with the intention of freeing ourselves from the tight grip of heteronormative thinking or, rather, the belief that all in the world are heterosexual unless s/he or they disclose otherwise.[30]

This kind of work does not only mean making the case for queerness; it also involves an open assault on the previous order:

We are committed to...doing the work required to dismantle cisgender privilege and uplift Black trans folk....
We are committed to embracing and making space for
trans brothers and sisters to participate and lead.[31]

Over and over again, we see that the world where every person is
either a man or a woman and lives according to God's creational design
is a world that must be "dismantled," in the verbiage of BLM. It is a
world where activists must work together to overthrow the hegemony
of "heteronormativity." These are not dispassionate recommenda-
tions; this is a battle plan and a war cry. It is not merely charting a
new genderfluid and sexually liberated path; it is also a willful and
concentrated rejection of the old path. Society should not be structured
according to manhood, womanhood, and the normalcy of what we
call heterosexuality. Society should in truth be structured around
queerness, fluidity, and polysexuality.

All this means that traditional men feel out of place and under
siege. They struggle to make sense of the conditions this pervasive
ideology creates. They know they do not fit into it, but they also know
they have little choice but to live in it. Everything seems reversed from
the way it should be: Boys look and act like girls. Girls look and act
like boys. Children grow up without any stable conception of boyhood
or girlhood. Hospitals founded to offer genuine medical care now perform mastectomies on children. Girls take drugs to try to stall puberty;
boys undergo treatments in an effort to develop female anatomy.
Androgyny becomes the norm, both in identity and appearance.

In such a mindset, the markers, practices, and appearance of
traditional manhood are cast aside. Boys having a boyish haircut,
dressing in a uniquely boyish way, striving to emulate their fathers
in how they walk and talk and shake hands, learning a distinctly

masculine way of life—all of this is not only not practiced, but actively opposed.

Factor #5: The Growth of Fear Culture and the Loss of Risk Culture

Some years ago, the late journalist Irving Kristol offered a salient critique of what he called "bourgeois society." It was, he asserted,

> organized for the convenience and comfort of common men and women, not for the production of heroic, memorable figures. It is a society interested in making the best of this world, not in any kind of transfiguration, whether through tragedy or piety.[32]

This is one of the most insightful analyses of modern America I have ever encountered. Once one sees our society in this light, one cannot see it any other way. Heroism is out; comfort is in.

This trend has only accelerated in recent years. The supposed threat of COVID-19 led to a global lockdown and a transformation of life across the world. COVID was and is a real illness and has affected many people. But it was not remotely the threat it was initially said to be, and even early recovery rates told a different story than that which many government officials passed along. What most concerns us for the purposes of this book, however, is the culture surrounding COVID. To put it simply, COVID exposed what an idol safety has become to many. Having lost the teleological and the theological, we are left with the immanent. The flourishing of *shalom*, the God-centered existence, does not concern many in the West, instead, the immediacy of survival occupies our every waking thought. God is a small thing to us, but our health looms above all as our greatest concern.

We could say we all live in a fear culture now. Our lives play in the key of fear. If you paid even minimal attention to public declarations and directives the last few years, you saw bureaucratic fear culture operating at a fever pitch. We were to fear the virus; fear standing near one another; fear not washing our hands; fear not wearing a mask; fear someone else's sneeze; fear travel; fear playgrounds; fear beaches; fear gathering for church; fear school; fear restaurants; fear most anything and everything. The rationale for all this fear came at us fast and furiously, bearing the weight of government edicts under the bland but all-consuming banner of "public health," while scientistic mobs did much of the work by shaming any who dared study the data, ask thoughtful questions, and not immediately receive every directive as gospel truth. We were not supposed to live in hope, confidence, stability, or peace; our world transitioned into a totalitarian darkness, and fear culture took hold in all its corners.

This trend did not just emerge. Irving Kristol saw it developing fifty years ago. But the medical, scientistic, and political fields all combined in an unprecedented way in 2020, as we all saw what truly matters most in our time: health. Bowing to the idol of health, we seek safety as the very *telos* of our days.

But strong men do not innately crave safety over everything else. It is true that men must be wise. But wisdom does not entail that men never take risks. God has given men an inner yearning to build, steward, stretch, grow, advance, and multiply. They do not want a cause that shrinks their life to nothing; men crave a higher calling that taxes and changes them and blesses others. Men not only want this; men need this.

Factor #6: The Loss of Work and Meaningful Endeavors

Men, as we saw in Chapter 1, are dropping out of the workforce in precipitous numbers, just as they are dropping out of school. The two trends are connected. Not every man needs to go to college, but for a good number of them, college serves as a helpful onramp to the world of work. Men who shift out of a vocational mindset into a recreational one, or simply an unplugged one, do not set themselves up for success; they set themselves and their loved ones up for further struggle and even failure.

Here again, COVID accelerated this trend. It was a terrible idea to lock healthy people down under the guise of keeping them safe. This was bad for most everyone, and especially bad for men, who need meaningful work in order to flourish. Men, as we shall see later on, were made to work. Leisure and rest are good; God Himself rested on the seventh day from all His labors (Genesis 1:31). But men do well when they have meaningful endeavors before them. It is a vital part of the good life, and it enables men to provide for their families, thus honoring God's design for them. In normal terms, women were not made to provide for their families; men were.

But our culture has communicated the opposite in numerous ways. Men should be safe instead of working; men should lean back so women can lean in and wear the provisional pants in the family; boys fit poorly into the cramped confines of the modern educational system and should be medicated so they can sit still; when men lead, they only mess things up, as their inherent aggression and competitiveness creates conflict, pain, and strife; the very model of men as providers signals that women are helpless, so that model should be jettisoned; we need to pursue equity and inclusivity today, not summon boys to be leaders. In these ways and many others, men hear a chorus of negativity that builds into a coherent message: *Drop back. Step aside. Stop advancing. You are outmoded. The future is female. We do not need you. Even more than this. We do not want you.*

In such a vicious climate, some men lash out, but many simply disappear. They retreat to the basement, to the garage, to the local bar, to video games for hour after hour after hour, to sports and lesser pursuits. Their avocations become their vocations; their hobbies become their life's center. They grow either listless and disengaged from serious things, or zealous and perpetually switched on toward smaller things. They are not a hero to anyone; they have lost the engine that drives their hourly existence; they have no greater cause to be a part of, even anonymously; they have no greater purpose at all and end up drifting through life, forgotten and miserable.

In such a climate, young men will become obsessed with unserious things, and thus will lose interest rapidly in serious things. This was true before COVID, as phones and computers largely took over our lives; it has only heightened since, as many young men were literally forced to stay home and spend hour upon hour on screens.

We must note that the society that fails to train boys to work is the society that seals its own demise. Work is not just earning a paycheck; it is a huge part of what gives manhood dignity and promise. All this is under threat today, though. Not working is the new working.

Factor #7: The Growth of Woke Cancel Culture

While I was growing up, it seemed like a middle space existed in American life. We could debate ideas without being marginalized and attacked for them. Today, however, much of the mainstream culture emanating from our universities, political bodies, businesses, and entertainment outlets has gone "woke." Wokeness represents the full bloom of what used to be called "political correctness." The word "woke" means that you are "awake" to the state of systemic racism and pervasive injustice in a given society. In the last decade or so, wokeness has become—with neopaganism—the dominant ideology in the West.

As I wrote in my book *Christianity and Wokeness*, wokeness has seeped into every facet of our public and private lives. Built on of the back of Marxism, wokeness trains its guns on majority groups, reading them as the oppressors of minorities. The grid by which woke folks work is an "intersectional" one, rooted in the idea that majority groups wield power over minority groups, fostering "systemic injustice." This form of oppression does not owe to explicit policies or acts or declarations; it is baked into the nature of society. Straight people oppress sexual minorities; able-bodied people oppress the disabled; in America and the West, "white" people oppress racial minorities; the wealthy oppress the poor; parents oppress their children; and on it goes. Life becomes an exercise in victimhood, unending blame, and identity politics.

Wokeness has had ten thousand terrible effects. For one, it promotes a victim/victimizer mentality. Sinners sin against one another and cause real pain—but in fundamental terms, we are not victims in Adam; we are all criminals, fellow sinners who hate God and rebel against Him. But a woke victim's mentality influences many to evade responsibility for their lives. It trains us to claim victim status and never own up to our failures and shortcomings. When men adopt such a mindset, they lose their way.

Woke voices do not often tell men they are victims, though (unless it means telling them they are victims of "toxic masculinity"). Typically, woke voices tell men they are victimizers who cannot escape this evil identity. Simply *being* a straight white male is seen as hostility by many in our culture, regardless of one's beliefs. As those who have and have had power and authority, men inherently oppress others. There is no real solution for this condition but for men to "confess their privilege," apologize for their toxicity, and fall silent.

The woke have tied such a problematic identity to the political specter of Trumpism. For our purposes, it is enough to note that simply voting for Trump meant the voter in question was perceived as being deeply morally compromised. Voting for him, the woke have argued, constituted support for all kinds of evil: white supremacy, the aforementioned toxic masculinity, and patriarchal oppression among them. Never mind that many Trump voters condemned those sins in no uncertain terms; simply casting one's vote in a conservative or Republican direction is now alleged to support fascism itself. In opposing their view of totalitarianism, the woke—perhaps unwittingly—have become totalitarian. Only they have a right to participate in a free society; those who do not have the right views destabilize it and so must lose their voice, their vote, and increasingly their constitutional rights.

Wokeness has played a major role in the chilling of free speech. We have seen this in many areas of our society. The Daily Wire's Ben Shapiro was shouted down many times on college campuses, and even barred from speaking at schools altogether. Many, many people were banned on Twitter and shadowbanned on other platforms for voicing views that went against elite narratives (shadowbanning is when social media administrators restrict one's posts so they don't reach the usual audience, usually without the person knowing it's happening). Professors and teachers lost jobs for not going with the current gender orthodoxy and using the "preferred pronouns" of "transgender" students. Book contracts were cancelled due to the author's promotion of conservative ideas.

The list of abuses of free speech, and free thought more broadly, could go on and on. There is an ocean of repression of speech and thought that has occurred in the last few decades that we could not quantify even if we tried. While everyone suffers in such poisoned climates, men suffer most. Boys communicate less fluidly than girls do; they need help, oftentimes, in developing the ability to voice their views. Many boys have to be coaxed into speaking up so others can hear them. Given the close organic connection between thinking well and speaking clearly, it is no small matter for boys to grow in their verbal powers. If they do not, they will be unable to lead.

Boys need training and discipline, but they also need to be able to speak freely, challenge one another in healthy ways, sort things out, declare their thoughts, exchange views and debate without rancor, and live in the joy of freedom. Today, however, "cancel culture" driven by woke ideologues has traded genuine learning for rote indoctrination. Everyone is worse off for it, but boys are particularly stunted in such an environment.

Conclusion

As I heard shouted in Washington, D.C., do all men lie? Yes, they do. So do all women. But our current climate all too often convicts only men and leaves them without any real hope. Indeed, as we have seen, manhood is not under attack from a vaguely defined "systemic" point of view, but from clear and identifiable sources—with Marxists, feminists, and gender activists leading that charge. The push to deconstruct the natural family continues in our day and entails the loss of a father for many children. Beyond this, various negative conditions of society work against men's prosperity. Problematizing their risk-taking nature calls into question the inborn instincts of men—instincts that can be used for good. Taking work away from a populace affects men immediately, for they are made to work. Inhibiting free speech shuts men down from speaking their mind—a necessary stage in masculine development and one that boys often struggle to negotiate.

As we shall see, however, men are not actually hopeless. They need great help, even the saving grace of God, but they are not outmoded. They are not consigned to the dustbin of history. The age of men is not over; the end of men is not upon us. The critics, naysayers, and gender theorists are wrong. Our task is not to revive men for their own selfish triumph, but to strengthen them by helping them not become lost men, soft men, exaggerated men, or angry men as God works and moves.

To that great end we now turn.

CHAPTER 3

The Foundation of Strong Manhood: Genesis 1–3

We need a generation of men who are alert to danger, who stand firm in the faith, who are courageous with the Word of God, uncompromising and strong.

John MacArthur

Daniel Haydel was returning home, exhausted, from a long night shift. It was 3:11 a.m. As a sheriff's deputy in Gonzales, Louisiana, Haydel had just completed twelve hours on the job. As he turned into his driveway, he received a distress call: a truck was sinking into a local bayou, and several adults and children were in it. Without a further thought, Haydel raced toward the scene, struggling in the nighttime fog and rain to find the sinking vehicle. Finally, with some help, he found it. He jumped onto the sinking truck and began smashing the back window.

Haydel took no regard for his own safety in his moment of heroism. He reacted in a state of high energy and surging adrenaline. Without such factors, he likely could not have saved anyone. In the moment, though, he did not stop to consider the odds. As the *Gonzales Weekly Citizen* reported,

He broke a car window with his fist and, assisted by additional deputies and firefighters, removed two children (ages 3 and 4), and a 24-year-old female to the bank of the canal, where CPR was administered.

The story continued: "While administering help, Haydel fractured his wrist in his efforts."[1]

Haydel pulled two adults and two children to safety. Sadly, two of those he saved later died. During a press conference, Haydel showed no triumph over the lives he heroically saved—he only broke down over those he lost. "I was called to do this job," he told the reporters. "It was . . . it was something I had to do."[2]

Haydel's heroism resurfaces the Hero Test I mentioned in the Introduction. We know we need men like this—strong men who stand up and sacrifice their interests for others. But as a society, we have lost the script for forming such men. In fact, as we have observed, many outlets and institutions *want* us to jettison the script for strong manhood. In a culture like this, how do we form this kind of man? This is a very big question, and yet very few people are trying to answer it today.

In a common-grace way, we are thankful when non-Christian men strive to lift other men up. Unbelievers can see some truths and offer some practical help to boys and young men. But the source of true wisdom is not to be found in any lost person. The book that defines manhood and gives men the guidance they need is the Word of God. The Bible is not a convenient accessory for manhood; it gives us God's truth, and where the Bible speaks to a subject, it speaks authoritatively and sufficiently.

The Word teaches us much about manhood, and so we may take great joy and comfort in this: We have God's own mind on what men are and must be. Manhood, as Genesis 1 and 2 show, was created by

God for His glory. Many voices speak to manhood, but God's voice is the one we must have and must hear.

God's Call to Strong Manhood in Genesis 1 and 2

On the sixth day, God made man in His own image. This means that before we understand humankind as having a body, emotions, or psyche, we must understand humankind as a spiritual race. We are made by God for God. We are made to know God. God is not supposed to be a distant factor in our recessed memories; He is supposed to be the central reality of our existence. We are not evolved dust; we are not advanced apes; we are not byproducts of randomness. No, there is a Creator who made us. We are creatures underneath the rule of God. God is the King of all the earth, and God made the earth to display His glory.

It is not the birds, mountains, or salamanders that most display God's greatness: It is the human race, man and woman, each made in the image of God. The man was made first as the image, and the woman was made from the man. Both the man and the woman thus have God-given dignity and worth. Humanity does not have to prove its worth or earn its keep in order to justify ongoing existence. Humanity has been given value, meaning, and hope by God Himself.

God made the man in His image (Genesis 1:26).[3] He called His special creation to have "dominion" over the rest of creation, including all that dwells in the sea, on the earth, and in the air (v. 26). God then "blessed" the man and woman, indicating His exclusive favor on them (v. 28). Then God charged them to "be fruitful and multiply and fill the earth and subdue it," following this by repeating the call to rule and dominion (v. 28).

Against an evolutionary mindset, we see in Scripture that humanity is the opposite of a purposeless race. We all have a reason to exist. We human beings were fashioned by God, invested with all sorts of ability and agency from Him, and are called to live in a Godlike way. By this I mean that God created and worked and stewarded creation, then gave us that same charge. God filled and populated the earth, then called us to fill and populate the earth. God loved beauty and the diversity of a world humming with life, then allowed us to love beauty and relish the wonder of this realm.

We learn much about manhood in particular in Genesis 2:7: The Lord made the man, Adam, first, forming him from the dust of the ground, breathing into his nostrils the breath of life. The Lord planted a garden in Eden and put the man there (v. 8). Adam was thus a gardener and a forester. Put differently, he was a steward, made to bring the created order to fruition. He lived in a paradise, surrounded by trees that were both "pleasant to the sight and good for food" (v. 9). The Tree of Life itself was in Eden, symbolizing the presence and blessing of God. There was also the Tree of the Knowledge of Good and Evil, which we shall say more about shortly.

Work and Keep the Garden

Eden was an altogether lovely place, a masterpiece of God's handiwork. It was Adam's home, and the Lord gave it to him to honor, cultivate, and defend. We see as much in Genesis 2:15–17, where the Lord speaks directly to the man:

> The LORD God took the man and put him in the garden
> of Eden to work it and keep it. And the LORD God com-
> manded the man, saying, "You may surely eat of every tree
> of the garden, but of the tree of the knowledge of good and
> evil you shall not eat, for in the day that you eat of it you
> shall surely die."

Adam received two directives from God. He had to work Eden, and he had to cultivate it. This is just one sentence in our English Bibles, and just two verbs in Hebrew.[4] But in these two words we find a key part of the call on every man's life.

Men are made for work, we see first. They are not made for idleness or passivity. Men are not made to get out of doing anything meaningful by any means necessary. No, they are called to work and are constituted for it. By this I mean that men's very biology fits with the divine mandate. We will discuss men's bodily design later on, but for now, it is enough to note that the man's body fits his vocation. He is a worker, made for action, made for stewarding Eden. Beyond this, he is made to provide for his family. Eve is not the one placed first in Eden to work it; she will play a great role in taking dominion of the earth, but it is Adam who has the call to work and thus to provide for his family.

Men do not naturally crave a listless life. They want a big mission. They want work to do. Men desire this because God made them to want it. Nor did God give Adam a single plant to tend—He gave him an entire garden-forest to steward and shepherd. This was a mission of dominion—exhilarating, expansive, exciting. This is what every man after Adam wants, too. Men do not want something small to live for. They can be indoctrinated that way, or lose their sense of meaning, but fundamentally, men yearn for something big to do. They want a mission that will consume them, even if their part in that work is not the lead role.

But just as Adam had to *take dominion*, so he also had to *keep dominion*. What he cultivated, he had to protect. We see that Adam was made not only for provision, but for protection. The two go hand in hand. Though Eden was as of yet untroubled, trouble was coming. "Watch out!" God effectively told Adam in Genesis 2:15. "Do not fall asleep." This word of warning applies not merely to

Adam but to men today. God has made us protectors, and so we are to put ourselves in harm's way on behalf of the innocent. Men must constantly be on the lookout in our own lives, homes, communities, churches, and societies.

Even as God calls Adam to strength in no uncertain terms, He also directs and then warns him in Genesis 2:16–17. Adam can eat from every tree except the Tree of the Knowledge of Good and Evil. Eating from that tree will bring death.

We learn much about God's character in these prescriptions. Against the stingy and angry portrait of God that skeptics and atheists give us, the Bible quotes Him as being stunningly generous in verse 16:

> "You may surely eat of every tree of the garden, but of the
> tree of the knowledge of good and evil you shall not eat, for
> in the day that you eat of it you shall surely die."

There is an entire forest of blessing before Adam that God has made, and He invites him to partake of it all.

Marry and Hold Fast

All this Adam hears from God. His duty is not to make up his own path or express his authentic self. His duty, quite simply, is to obey God and keep covenant with Him. At this point we learn about Adam's next role: he is to be a husband and eventually a father, as Genesis 2:18–25 reveals:

> Then the LORD God said, "It is not good that the man
> should be alone; I will make him a helper fit for him." Now
> out of the ground the LORD God had formed every beast
> of the field and every bird of the heavens and brought them

to the man to see what he would call them. And whatever the man called every living creature, that was its name. The man gave names to all livestock and to the birds of the heavens and to every beast of the field. But for Adam there was not found a helper fit for him. So the LORD God caused a deep sleep to fall upon the man, and while he slept took one of his ribs and closed up its place with flesh. And the rib that the LORD God had taken from the man he made into a woman and brought her to the man. Then the man said,

"This at last is bone of my bones and flesh of my flesh; she shall be called Woman, because she was taken out of Man."

Therefore a man shall leave his father and his mother and hold fast to his wife, and they shall become one flesh. And the man and his wife were both naked and were not ashamed.

The only "not good" element of Eden was Adam's aloneness (v. 18). He could not fulfill the dominion mandate by himself. He certainly could not multiply image-bearers on the earth by himself. Further, according to Almighty God, he needed a "helper."[5] This shows us that men are not all-sufficient in themselves. Many men need wives. This woman Adam was to have would bring real abilities, capacities, and blessings to him and to the creation. She would have certain strengths he did not have. Her gifting as a helper is no threat to him; her gifting according to her God-given role is a profound blessing to him, one he welcomes and enables in every way he can.

So the Lord made the woman for Adam from his rib (v. 21). The consummate Artist, the Lord created Eve in perfect wisdom and brought her to him (v. 22). When Adam saw her, he exclaimed in delight words to the effect of: This *at last* was his helpmate, *Ishah*, taken out of his own body (v. 23). The two were distinct as man and woman, but united in this garden marriage ceremony by God.[6] Their unity ran so deep that Adam saw her as bone of his bone and flesh of his flesh. This in fact is what their sexual union would picture: *one flesh* (v. 24). This one-flesh reality does indeed speak to the beauty of God's design for sex between one husband and one wife in marriage. But the union captured here goes beyond physical togetherness and speaks to the joining of souls as well as bodies, intimacy of the closest and most joyful kind.

Lead and Love

This passage helps us understand the nature of men. Many men have a strong sexual drive. It is because God has made us this way, in part so that we will leave our childhood family and form a new one. Understood from this foundation, it is good and right that a man desires the gift of sex in the covenant of marriage. The Bible, after all, does not only say "no" to sin; it says, still louder, "yes!" to God's goodness and grace. So we must steward this instinct well and with God's help; we must know that this capacity can be used for great good, but also for great evil.

As a gift of God, sex enfleshes the love of one man for one woman. It shows us how great the intimacy is in marriage, the institution made by God to display the greatest love there is: the love of Christ for His Church (Ephesians 5:22–33). For these and related reasons, he who finds a wife finds a good thing, a Heaven-sent thing. While treasuring all these benefits of marriage, our union does not depend on our feelings; in times of pain and times of happiness, we stubbornly "hold fast" to our wife (v. 24). She does not keep us with her; we embrace her and never let her go. We must be men who make commitments and then keep them. The greatest one we can make in this life is to our wife.

All this leads to the third major dimension of biblical manhood: *leadership*. The man must lead by the call of God. The woman does not leave father and mother initially; it is the man who does. The woman does not hold fast to her husband; it is the man who holds fast to her. Genesis 2 is giving us a clear sign of the man's leadership role in marriage; he has authority from God to act so as to pursue marriage and remain in it, for holding fast is not a one-time event but a lifelong commitment empowered by the grace of God.

The man, the New Testament teaches, has headship over his wife (1 Corinthians 11:3).[7] He is her head, her authority, and she finds her earthly leader in him and no other man. This is never an excuse for a man to sin or do what he wants just because he is the leader; the call to leadership, on the contrary, is a challenging and never-ceasing call to holiness, love, and self-rule.

As we live in this pattern—never perfectly, but as a pursuit—God intends that men and women alike would know happiness and blessing. This is what resulted for Adam and Eve: they were naked and unashamed (v. 25). This reminds us that God is not a prude. God does not only want us to worship Him only for an hour or two per week. God set all of life up to be an exercise in doxology and worship. Our entire existence is spiritual. This means that every moment of our existence is a moment we can give to God. Every good thing we taste can cause us to praise Him. This is the kind of "unashamed" happiness that Adam and Eve know at the end of the sixth day, sketched for us in Genesis 2. It is a day, truly, that teaches us much about who God created us to be as men.

The Strong Man Turned Lost Man: Manhood in Genesis 3

But all God's good purposes for Adam came to naught. As Genesis 3:1–7 records, the man called to be a strong man by God did not heed His word. He became a very different type instead: the *lost man*. Adam, to put it simply, disappeared. So we see in the text:

Now the serpent was more crafty than any other beast of the field that the LORD God had made. He said to the woman, "Did God actually say, 'You shall not eat of any tree in the garden'?" And the woman said to the serpent, "We may eat of the fruit of the trees in the garden, but God said, 'You shall not eat of the fruit of the tree that is in the midst of the garden, neither shall you touch it, lest you die.'" But the serpent said to the woman, "You will not surely die. For God knows that when you eat of it your eyes will be opened, and you will be like God, knowing good and evil." So when the woman saw that the tree was good for food, and that it was a delight to the eyes, and that the tree was to be desired to make one wise, she took of its fruit and ate, and she also gave some to her husband who was with her, and he ate. Then the eyes of both were opened, and they knew that they were naked. And they sewed fig leaves together and made themselves loincloths.

We cannot attempt a long breakdown of this passage. Instead, we observe five truths about the fall of humanity as captured here.

First, the serpent engages the woman first. He goes around the man and does not honor creation order; the man called to "guard" or "keep" the garden is left unengaged. Second, in verse 1, the serpent lies about what God said, for God's first word to Adam was that he could eat from *any* tree in Eden save one.

Third, the serpent directly counters the true word of God in verse 4. He tells Eve both that God is wrong—"You will not surely die"—and that He is wrongly withholding godlikeness from the man and the woman (4–5). Satan's chief stratagem is to foster doubt about God's character; he will use any lie he can to drive us to doubt and distrust God. Fourth, the woman stops thinking with a sound mind and instead follows the serpent's guidance. Doing so means she sees the tree through the prism of pleasure without piety—in a fleshly way, not a faith-filled way (v. 6).

Fifth, and most significantly for our study, we discover the world's first *lost man* in this sad scene. To be precise, Adam was present as Eve talked with Satan. But for all purposes, he abandoned his duties. He did not speak; he did not act in any virtuous way; he did nothing except follow his wife's lead (v. 6). He should have refuted the serpent's lies and protected his wife from them. But he did no such thing. God made Adam to be the strong man, but Adam simply disappeared in the face of this evil.

In this sorry scene, we see why we all sin. It shows us the way of the *lost man*. We grasp why men are tempted to tune out, drop out, and disappear. Adam did. He heard from God Himself that he should step up and defend Eden and protect his wife. We should not think that the pre-Fall garden was an impenetrable fortress. God had already told Adam in so many words that a grave threat was headed his way. But in his great hour of testing, Adam did not rise up in courage. He did not meet the threat as it came to his territory. He shrank back. His wife leaned in, but Adam opted out.

This disappearance did not only mean he did not act; it meant that he effectively thrust his wife into the serpent's onslaught. Abandonment is not merely abandonment; it is that, but it is also much more. It is leaving one's loved ones to face the bared fangs of the devil himself, unprotected and unguarded. The *lost man* may think he is simply walking away from his problems, but in truth, he only amplifies them for himself and his loved ones. Vanishing might feel good, but it heals nothing. It only brings worse suffering than before.

Try as Adam might, he could not actually disappear. God's own actions make this painfully clear. The Lord visited Eden and made a beeline for the man, calling out to him, "Where are you?" (v. 9).

Adam responded by shifting blame: he first blamed Eve, then God, and only then—when he had minimized his own failing—did he name himself (v. 12). Here we see not just Adam's sin, but our own sinful instincts as men. When challenged, and even when caught in wickedness, we get defensive. We make excuses. We ourselves try to disappear, so to speak.

But God made it impossible for Adam to disappear again. Because he had listened to his wife and eaten the forbidden fruit, breaking God's commandment, God cursed the ground (v. 17) for Adam. Previously, the earth would yield its fruits willingly; now, it would produce "thorns and thistles," and the man's labor to work and provide would break his body down into an eventual state of dust (v. 18–19). Going forward, work in Eden would be hard; it would be painful; it would culminate in death. None of this means that God hates work or wants us to despise it, but it does mean that men must now work under a shadow all their days—toiling, with aching bodies, burdened in many respects.

This is all because of sin. So it was for Adam; so it is for us. As we read Genesis 3, we need to remember: you and I are not better than Adam. You and I *are* Adam. We are sinners because he became a sinner (1 Corinthians 15:22).[8] In Adam, we fail and falter and sin, and thus, we all are by nature wicked. Though we face real trials in this fallen realm, someone else is not our greatest problem; *we* are our greatest problem. Indwelling sin, and not anything we have experienced, however awful, is our foremost adversary.[9] Self-esteem, therapy, and positive thinking cannot solve this situation. We need something stronger. We need *redemption*.

Thankfully, God is in the redemption business. Genesis 3 makes this clear: the Lord promised the serpent that his reign of sin and death would meet its match. God would send His "seed" or "offspring" in years to come, and "he shall bruise your head, and you shall bruise his heel" (Genesis 3:15). This is God's promise of deliverance from the devil. It means He will win the great conflict with Satan. God would send a warrior in due time to destroy the devil's power over believers by atoning for our sins. He would take God's wrath for us. He would die in our place. He would suffer so that we could go free (see Isaiah 53).[10]

What encouragement this gives us who are tempted to embrace the way of the *lost man*. The devil had his day in Eden, and even now he rages against us—but he will lose in the end. After all, God has His best man on the job.

Conclusion

This is the kind of man we need today. We do not need any more *lost men*, tempted as we all are to drop out and flee responsibility. We need the Strong Man, Jesus Christ. We need men who reflect Him in their daily lives. Like Daniel Haydel in the Louisiana bayou at 3 a.m., we need men who do not leave it to others to do the hard work and the dirty jobs. We need men who will step up on others' behalf, leading, protecting, and providing whether they are well-rested or totally exhausted. We need men who are not only *willing* to suffer and—if necessary—die in the line of fire, but men who are *ready* to answer the call of courage.

As we have seen already in this project, men find themselves in a war today. In many respects, this war is upon us without our even knowing it, let alone wanting it. We have not chosen our station or the era in which we live. We have been placed here. We have been called to be men in this particular time, facing these particular challenges. We can reject this war, bemoan it, or try to escape through one fantasy after another. Or we can declare war on the war, and pray to be strong men in an age of compromised men. The distress call has gone out, and loudly. The question before us is, quite simply, this: Will we answer it or not?

CHAPTER 4

The Foundation of Manhood: Old Testament Men

*Our good Lord and Master ought not to be
followed by cowards.*

Charles Spurgeon

I t was just a boy standing atop a shed. But the image immediately got my attention.

The backstory is a little complicated, but here's the gist of it: A homeschooling mother encountered some opposition from her fourteen-year-old son over reading *Hamlet*. Seeing that this challenge could become a growth opportunity, she gave him the option of sticking with Shakespeare or building a shed; he chose the shed. He got building manuals, learned "construction math," and singlehandedly built it. Afterward, the boy climbed to its peak and his mother snapped a picture.

This little anecdote went so much against the grain, I could not help but reach out to Julie, the mother in question. I wanted to know where she got such wisdom to steer her son. Here's part of what she wrote to me. It's marvelous stuff:

> A teacher, my husband Tom reads a book called *The Iceberg Hermit* aloud to his students (it is sadly out of print). It tells

the story of a teenage boy who thinks he's stupid because he does so poorly in school, but when shipwrecked in the arctic (with only a pocket Bible his mother had made him promise to read every day) he summons up skills he never knew he had in order to survive and eventually be rescued. One of the questions my husband asks his students is, "What skills do you have that you would be able to use to survive if you were in this situation?" Frequently, the students say "none."[1]

Our boys need discipling and training, as this family is providing. But even when they have it, we cannot really know how our boys will turn out. In this chapter, we look at several examples of manhood, both positive and negative, in the Old Testament, and find four types of men that boys could become. Having already seen Adam change from *strong man* to *lost man*, in this chapter, we will study Cain, a blessed man turned *angry man*. We next analyze Gideon, a *soft man* whom God emboldened and strengthened. Then, we consider Samson, who tragically preferred life as an *exaggerated man*. Finally, we trace the story of young David, a shepherd who became the deliverer of Israel—a *strong man* despite his sin.

In these portraits, we see what men are in their sin, what tempts them, and what they can become by the grace of God. By this reflection, we see our own possibilities, our own temptation toward various forms of deficient manhood, and the path to strong manhood that lies before all men.

An Angry Man: Cain

The first story we cover about manhood is as true as it is tragic. Immediately following their banishment from Eden, God gives Eve conception. As Genesis 4:1–7 shows, she bears a son, crediting her childbearing to the Lord (showing that she had faith in God). Cain comes first, then his brother Abel (v. 2). The text makes clear that the two brothers are quite different from one another in many ways:

> Now Abel was a keeper of sheep, and Cain a worker of the ground. In the course of time Cain brought to the LORD an offering of the fruit of the ground, and Abel also brought of the firstborn of his flock and of their fat portions. And the LORD had regard for Abel and his offering, but for Cain and his offering he had no regard. So Cain was very angry, and his face fell. The LORD said to Cain, "Why are you angry, and why has your face fallen? If you do well, will you not be accepted? And if you do not do well, sin is crouching at the door. Its desire is contrary to you, but you must rule over it."

Abel's offering pleased the Lord, while Cain's did not. It appears that this is because Abel brought the best of what he had: "the firstborn of his flock," which revealed a heart given over to God. Cain made no such offering, and when Abel's offering pleased the Lord, Cain showed the fruit of an evil heart: he "was very angry" with both God and Abel (v. 5). Here is where we see the first angry man emerging from Scripture. Cain did not battle or rule his anger; he let it rule him.

The Lord Himself spoke to Cain, warning him in stark terms about the course he was traveling. In His rebuke, we glean something about the nature of sin: sin is not a passive little presence in our world, tucked away in a closet somewhere. Sin is a viper in the grass; as God said to Cain, it was "crouching at the door," and it sought to rule him (v. 7). In the metaphor God uses, sin waits to pounce and can only be overcome if one meets it with great force.

How informative this is; how enlightening. The sins we repeatedly commit lie in wait for us. They will rule us if we do not rule them by the overmastering grace of God. This was God's warning to Cain, and it is His warning to us. We should take special heed to it if, like Cain, we have a propensity for sensitivity, defensiveness, and pride. The warning God gives Cain is a warning He gives to us, too. We also have a temper. We also feel self-pity and jealousy when we do poorly and others do well. We are all guilty here.

This means the way of the angry man is open before us, just as the way of the strong, godly man is open to us. It is terrifyingly easy for all of us to travel Cain's course. We are all sinners by nature, and sin crouches for us as it did for Cain. We can either fight sin through repentance and faith, or we can lean into our anger and approach life as an exercise in vengeance. Tragically, this was Cain's choice. When he and Abel went out into the field, "Cain rose up against his brother Abel and killed him" (v. 8).

When the Lord asked Cain where Abel was, he denied being his "brother's keeper," but the Lord's response shows otherwise (v. 9). Cain slew Abel, and his blood shouted "from the ground" (v. 10). So the Lord sentenced Cain, making him a fugitive and a nomad (v. 12)—but still protected him so that he could not be killed, showing him kindness, and Cain settled "east of Eden" (v. 16).

The story of Cain and Abel needs to get our attention. It should remind us how easy it is to let evil rule us. The type of the *angry man* is real and deadly. We all know this type; many of us have strong tempers. There is righteous anger, yes; but for many men, our temper will be one of our primary foes throughout our lives. If we do not control our tempers by God's power, they will cause great pain for us and others.

This is what is happening today as some young men without fathers unleash terrible violence on the innocent. They do so in many cases because they are deeply angry, and they have no means by which to rein in their rage. They remind us that the way of the *angry man* is not hard for us to adopt. It is all too easy, and all too devastating.

The Wavering but Faithful Heart of Gideon

The next man we study had a very different reaction to evil. Gideon was a wavering man who hailed from a compromised Israelite family. His father openly worshiped Baal and led the men in Gideon's town to do the same. Gideon himself harvested wheat at night so as not to draw the attention of the surrounding Midianites, enemies who menaced Israel continuously. Pastor John MacArthur describes this arduous undertaking:

> The process of beating out grain and separating it from the chaff normally took place out in the open, on a hilltop, where the breeze would blow the chaff away.[2]

Gideon, however, was "fearful that enemy marauders might spot him" and so "took cover in the quarried shelter of a winepress." This made his job difficult, "but at least his efforts would go undetected, or so he imagined."[3] Gideon hid from the Midianites, but he could not hide from God. When the Lord called him into service, the angel addressing him named him as a "mighty man of valor" (Judges 6:12). Here is great encouragement for struggling men: Even when we are weak, God calls us out of our sin and into His divine strength to do what we ourselves would never think possible.

The Lord next called Gideon to destroy his father Joash's idolatrous altars to demonic gods. Gideon did so and built an offering to the true God in their place, honoring the Lord's directive. But he did not do this in the day; he did it in the middle of the night to avoid detection (Judges 6:25–27). Though Joash could have led the whole town to riot against Gideon, he stood up for his son, showing that courageous actions often yield positive results (vv. 28–32). Just as cowardice begets cowardice, courage begets courage.

The Lord then put Gideon to work in a still greater way, calling him to gather the people of God against the Midianites and Amalekites, who marched on Israel to destroy it. Gideon, cloaked in the power of the Spirit, did so, and several tribes responded (vv. 33–35).

At this point, we might think that Gideon armed up and went straight into battle. After all, the Lord had brought him through a serious test already. But this is not what Gideon did. He put God to the test, asking Him to prove that He would fight for him by putting dew on a fleece, but keeping the surrounding ground dry. The Lord did this, but Gideon's anxiety did not subside. He next asked the Lord to make the fleece dry and the ground around it wet. The Lord again did as Gideon asked (vv. 36–40). In this strange scene, we see the Lord's tremendous patience on full display. He could have nuked Gideon, or at least subjected him to a withering critique. But he did neither. He honored Gideon's fearful requests and proved to this timid but God-worshiping man that He cared for him and would help him.

But the Lord did not stop there. He led Gideon in what we can only describe as a patient and kind manner. As so often happened in divine-human interactions in the Old Testament, the true God showed massive restraint in engaging His wayward people.

But the Lord also decided to unveil the great force of His all-conquering will: Gideon amassed an army of thirty-two thousand men, which the Lord then pared down to ten thousand (Judges 7:1–3). Following this, the Lord made a second major cut. He had Gideon do a test and kept for his army only those men who lapped water, "putting their hands to their mouths" to drink (v. 6). This left all of three hundred men, the final number of Gideon's army. These men, it must be said, represented a serious batch, as their habit of raising water to their mouths likely indicated that they warily scanned the horizon as they drank.

With just three hundred men, the Lord sent Gideon's army into battle—but not before allowing Gideon to eavesdrop on a conversation in which an unnamed enemy soldier told his friend that God would defeat Midian through Gideon's sword (vv. 9–14). Again, the Lord took pains to encourage His fearful follower, showing great patience beyond what could reasonably be asked or expected. Nor did the Lord fail to keep His word. Gideon and his men rushed on the enemy force, and the Lord threw the Midianites into confusion. At the sound of the Israelite trumpets, "the LORD set every man's sword against his comrade and against all the army" (v. 22). On that day, the Lord routed the enemy forces.

The story of Gideon should encourage us all tremendously. We see nothing less than the heart of God for struggling men in this story, for the Lord works with Gideon, building up his faith amidst multiple bouts of anxiety, and then pulling off a showstopper victory that demonstrates His mighty power. God does not rub His might in Gideon's face, but He does leave him (and us) breathless at the power of His greatness. The lesson is clear: God will use those pulled toward passivity to accomplish His perfect plan. Unlike an unkind world, which all too often roots against men, God will put those who are weak to work. He will not scorch them and dismiss them. He will use them to pull off almost inconceivable feats, magnifying His strength in their weakness.

But we should also receive a clear warning from Gideon's example: God made him strong, but Gideon's flesh encouraged him to embrace the way of the soft man. The soft man does not confront evil boldly and courageously. He lives a wavering life. He waffles in and out. He will not step forward in faith. Gideon is much like another Old Testament figure, Barak, who looked to a woman, Deborah, to mount up against evil forces (see Judges 4–5). Barak did go into battle, but only after much doubting and second-guessing.

Barak went further than Gideon, in fact. He asked a woman to play his role, and Deborah called him out for it:

And she said, "I will surely go with you. Nevertheless, the road on which you are going will not lead to your glory, for the LORD will sell Sisera into the hand of a woman." Then Deborah arose and went with Barak to Kedesh. (Judges 4:9).

As the text shows, Deborah did not celebrate Barak's fearfulness. She rightly shamed him for it. Like so many women today, she wanted Barak to act in strength, not weakness. But when he failed in this regard, she accepted responsibility.

Through Gideon and Barak, we men receive a stout biblical warning. Our culture, like our flesh, encourages us to adopt the way of the soft man today, but we must not. We are not to compete against women, but we should trust the Lord, pray when our hearts flutter, and lead in conviction and Godward hope. We should not excuse our weakness when we find it, as find it we shall. We should repent of softness—by which I mean cowardice and ungodly slowness to obey God.

Our culture encourages boys to be passive and girls to be leaders; it strives to take the aggressiveness and assertiveness from our sons. We must not let it. While training our boys to be gentle and kind, we should always point them to the need for courage, for action, for decisiveness, and for clarity of leadership. Anything less is failure—a failure to obey God and a failure to practice manhood as God formed it. This conviction is not merely something to teach, though; this conviction must be *lived*, modeled, and celebrated.

The Exaggerated Manhood of Samson

We have already found in Scripture the *lost man*, the *angry man*, and the *soft man*. Now, in the person of Samson, we discover the way of the *exaggerated man*.

Samson was blessed from birth with incredible strength. Raised under the Nazirite vow, he was called to grow his hair without cutting it, steer clear of dead bodies, and drink no wine. Samson truly is one of the Bible's most compelling characters, bursting onto the troubled pages of the book of Judges like a fictional hero whom God uses in profound ways despite his flaws. But Samson was no pretend character; he was all too real.

Everything about Samson was outsized. He was rash, impulsive, and lived according to what he saw and wanted. He was handsome, well-muscled, and outwardly impressive. Though called to be a judge of Israel, he chose to live largely by his own code. He did what he wanted and got what he desired, and so represents the ideal of men who want to live a fleshly existence and pay no consequences for it. Charles Spurgeon nails the character of Samson:

> Perhaps the extraordinary strength of his physical frame placed him under stronger temptation than is common to man: at any rate, he was peculiarly constituted, and seemed more like a wanton boy than a judge in Israel.[4]

From the start, he lived on the edge. He went down to enemy territory, where he saw a lovely Philistine girl. The text records his entitlement: "I saw one of the daughters of the Philistines at Timnah. Now get her for me as my wife" (Judges 14:2), he tells his father.

Samson was all impulse, no self-rule. Despite his poor character, the Lord was actually behind this, as destruction and mayhem would soon visit the Philistines (v. 4). We should not read the text as God's approval of Samson's request, but as the Lord using a flawed man in His wise plan, as He so often does.

Various shenanigans ensued. When threatened by a roaring lion, Samson killed it with his bare hands, as Judges 14:6 substantiates:

Then the Spirit of the LORD rushed upon him, and although he had nothing in his hand, he tore the lion in pieces as one tears a young goat. But he did not tell his father or his mother what he had done.

God Himself gave Samson this strength, another reminder that we can never claim strength in ourselves but must always look to the Lord for it. Later, when Samson went to get his wife, he walked by the same lion's carcass. Bees had built a hive in it and produced honey, and Samson without blinking ate it, not even bothering to use an implement to draw it from the lion's body (v. 9). That was Samson: he saw something, wanted it, and got it for himself. His Nazirite vow meant nothing to him; he lived an ancient version of a longstanding male fantasy, and not a healthy one.

The Lord nonetheless employed Samson to spectacular ends. The Philistines tried to overcome him, but again God acted through this man to thrash them:

When he came to Lehi, the Philistines came shouting to meet him. Then the Spirit of the LORD rushed upon him, and the ropes that were on his arms became as flax that has caught fire, and his bonds melted off his hands. And he found a fresh jawbone of a donkey, and put out his hand and took it, and with it he struck 1,000 men. (Judges 15:14–15)

Again, the text makes clear that Samson's evisceration of Israel's dread foes did not happen through his raw ability. Samson had natural strength, yes, but God favored him, and that accounted for his victory. The Spirit of the Lord worked on Samson, and not in a meek and mild way. Samson sliced through the enemies of God's people with a donkey's jawbone, not even using a sword or formal weapon of war. Again, we note, he violated his Nazirite vow by touching corpses. Samson lived his life rashly and would soon pay very dearly for it.

It was not an army that overcame the fearsome warrior: it was a woman. Samson had the natural urges of an alpha male and acted accordingly. His eyes drove him: in Gaza, "he saw a prostitute, and he went in to her" (Judges 16:1). Samson had no regard for God's law, holiness, and call on his life. His was a high-velocity, get-it-while-you-can existence. But he then met his match: Delilah.

Enlisted by the Philistines, the cunning Delilah tried to wear Samson down, entreating him over and over to tell her the secret of the source of his strength. Samson resisted, foiling the enemy's efforts three times by lying to Delilah. (Samson and Delilah show us what a poisonous relationship looks like.) But eventually, Samson tells Delilah the truth, she cuts his hair, and the Philistines capture him (Judges 16:19).

The Lord had left Samson, the text tells us; he was on his own, and immediately failed (v. 20). The man who lived by his eyes had them gouged out by his foes (v. 21).

But the God of Samson is a redeemer, as we have seen. He did not rescue Samson or return his sight, but He did restore his strength. Samson asked:

> "O Lord GOD, please remember me and please strengthen me only this once, O God, that I may be avenged on the Philistines for my two eyes." (Judges 16:28)

The Lord granted his request, as Samson, standing between two great pillars holding up the hall where the Philistines worshiped their demonic god Dagon,

> bowed with all his strength, and the house fell upon the lords and upon all the people who were in it. So the dead

whom he killed at his death were more than those whom
he had killed during his life. (v. 30)

The story of Samson is complex. It reminds us that God uses even
the stubborn and foolish in His perfect plans. Samson lived unwisely
and impulsively, operating by his base instincts and passions.

He lived a version of what some men still dream of thousands of
years later. A good number of men do in fact reject feminism, wokeness, and an androgynous order. They seek instead to be maximally
powerful; they want to bed women as they wish, and they want to do
whatever they want without consequence. They think themselves strong
men. Unfortunately, like Samson, they largely practice a counterfeit.

We see this with the rise of interest in men like former kickboxer
Andrew Tate. Tate is brash, bold, and lives an extravagant life. Many
young men follow his exploits on social media and YouTube. Men like
Tate will always draw a crowd in feminist contexts, because they cut
against the grain. Tate does stand for some traditional ideas, which
accounts for some of his popularity in an age of political correctness
run amok. But ultimately, he does not show men the way forward.
Feminism and transgenderism should not lead men to think that
misogyny and dominating women is the way forward. Men really
are under fire today, but we should not exaggerate our manhood in
response. Instead, we should embrace maturity, love wisdom, live
confidently in God, enjoy being a man, and die to self in the power
of Christ.

Samson is the original playboy. He had incredible strength, and
he lived a life any red-blooded man would admire in his sin. But in
Scripture, Samson stands as a cautionary tale, not a model to chase.
This is not because God wants us men to become weak or insipid.
He wants us to be strong, but not in a fleshly way. He wants us
to fight evil, but not for our own selfish purposes. He wants us to

marry a woman if called to marriage, but not to see women as conquests or trophies. He wants us to rise above the flesh, not indulge it.

In the end, Samson's example reminds us of our great need to pursue strength in God, not ourselves. Samson's story also displays the kindness of God in using selfish and stumbling creatures like us to glorify Himself. Even Samson, foolish as he could be, was not wasted. This should shape how we approach those drawn to the way of the exaggerated man. They should not be cancelled or hated; instead, we should preach the Gospel to them, call them to repentance, and ask the Lord to use them for His purposes, not their own. If God can use Samson, He can use many we might think are too far gone. Though there are definite limits to our strength, there are no limits to the redeeming reach of God's arm.

David: A Young Man Who Was a Strong Man

David is one of the most fascinating and encouraging men in the Bible. As we shall see, God used him to accomplish spectacular good. David is thus a model for us. But we must take note here: the true hero of the story of David vs. Goliath is not David, but God. In David's triumph, we see that God takes a man who is nothing in the world's eyes and gives him power to win an incredible victory. As we have observed already, we may be weak in ourselves, but God is strong and enables His people to be strong by His grace. This is truly one of the dominant themes of the entire Bible.

If you could have seen Goliath back in the day, you would have thought him unbeatable. Per 1 Samuel 17, he was about nine feet tall. His coat of armor alone weighed about 125 pounds. His spear was made of iron and weighed about fifteen pounds; it must have made a sickening thud when it went through a person, which it did often. Goliath roared against the Israelites, making the fight between the peoples not only a test of skill, but a test of manhood:

He stood and shouted to the ranks of Israel, "Why have
you come out to draw up for battle? Am I not a Philistine,
and are you not servants of Saul? Choose a man for yourselves, and let him come down to me. If he is able to fight
with me and kill me, then we will be your servants. But if
I prevail against him and kill him, then you shall be our
servants and serve us." And the Philistine said, "I defy the
ranks of Israel this day. Give me a man, that we may fight
together." (1 Samuel 17:8–10)

Goliath seems almost offended by the softness of the Israelite
army. He seems to want a challenger, and he openly dishonors the
army that will not come against him. The text tells us exactly why:
From King Saul all the way down to his men, the Israelites "were
dismayed and greatly afraid" when they heard Goliath's roaring challenge (1 Samuel 17:11).

In natural terms, this made sense. Goliath was not *artificially*
terrifying; he was *actually* terrifying. The mere sight of him made
one's blood cool to ice.

But there was a young man who did not fear him. David had
only gone to the battlefield that day in order to honor his father's
command to give his brothers some supplies. They were part of the
Israelite army, whereas young David was not. But when David heard
Goliath defy Israel, and in truth, defy Israel's God, something in him
sparked. Hearing the men talk about rewards, he asked:

"What shall be done for the man who kills this Philistine
and takes away the reproach from Israel? For who is this
uncircumcised Philistine, that he should defy the armies of
the living God?" (v. 26)

David's second question shows that he does not ultimately care about the rewards that will accrue to the man who kills Goliath. He cares most about the fact that Israel's God is being insulted. As pastor Grant Castleberry has well said, he cares about the honor of God above all.[5]

It does not take long for David to face opposition. His oldest brother shows clear signs of soft manhood. Like the rest of the army, he is not up for fighting Goliath, but he is willing to scorch his courageous little brother. Angrily, he asks David:

> "Why have you come down? And with whom have you left those few sheep in the wilderness? I know your presumption and the evil of your heart, for you have come down to see the battle." (v. 28)

The implication here is that David is nothing more than a combat tourist. This is what a soft man all too often does: he sneers at the strong man, trying to make himself feel better about his own cowardice.

David keeps moving.[6] Empowered by the grace of God, he does not let obstacles slow him down. Yet for all his vigor, he hears yet another discouraging word, this time from King Saul, who flatly dismisses him: "You are not able to go against this Philistine to fight with him, for you are but a youth, and he has been a man of war from his youth" (v. 33). Saul judges by sight; David lives by faith. David tells the king in no uncertain terms:

> "Your servant has struck down both lions and bears, and this uncircumcised Philistine shall be like one of them, for he has defied the armies of the living God." (v. 36)

He doubles down, in fact:

> "The LORD who delivered me from the paw of the lion and
> from the paw of the bear will deliver me from the hand of
> this Philistine." (v. 37)

Here is one of the Bible's most glowing pictures of what strong
men do. Strong men are not merely strong where others shrink back.
True strength is not found in sinful flesh; it is found in God. David is
not strong because he goes out to face Goliath; he is *already* strong
in the faith God developed in him while he was on the backside of
nowhere, tending sheep. That is why David was willing to walk
where no other Israelite would. He was a man of God. He feared
the Lord. He did not tremble before Goliath; he trembled before the
great and awesome God of Israel.

The giant next heaped shame on David, literally cursing him: "'Am
I a dog, that you come to me with sticks?' And the Philistine cursed
David by his gods" (v. 43). But David paid his evil trash-talking no
mind: "You come to me with a sword and with a spear and with a
javelin," he retorted, "but I come to you in the name of the LORD of
hosts, the God of the armies of Israel, whom you have defied" (v. 45).
David then gave Goliath a promise, as only a warrior would:

> "This day the LORD will deliver you into my hand, and I
> will strike you down and cut off your head. And I will give
> the dead bodies of the host of the Philistines this day to the
> birds of the air and to the wild beasts of the earth, that all
> the earth may know that there is a God in Israel, and that
> all this assembly may know that the LORD saves not with
> sword and spear. For the battle is the LORD's, and he will
> give you into our hand." (vv. 46–47)

If Goliath uttered the speech of Hell, David uttered the speech of Heaven. He promised victory, but did so in the tones of trust. It was "the Lord" who would give Goliath into David's hand. Goliath was armed with all the trappings of war; David was armed in the truth of God. Trusting in the Lord, he moved ahead fearlessly. What a display of strong godly manhood he put on before a watching audience! He did not merely stand there as Goliath drew near; he "ran quickly" to meet his foe (v. 48). He slung a single stone and hit the Philistine dead on the forehead, killing him instantly (v. 49). Then he took the giant's sword, administered a death blow, and cut off his head (v. 51).

What a display of strength. What a revelation of how God delights in working through the despised things of the earth to take down the high and mighty. Though imperfect, David is a model for us. While a sinner just like us, he shows us that strong men do not come in only one size or shape or look. Being a strong man of God is not about your genetics or looks; being a strong man is all about the favor and goodness of God. When God works in us, and when we depend on Him for strength, He delights in giving us what we need. He really does empower us, but always in such a way that His own divine strength takes center stage.

We see that by the grace of God, just one man with courage can change everything. After David cut off Goliath's head, the armies of Israel "rose with a shout" and savaged the wicked Philistines (v. 52). The effect of David's action was seismic, the equivalent of a militaristic earthquake. What a lesson for us, and what a call to us across the ages. We men must step up in the darkest times. We must not fear to be alone.

David is one of many examples of godly men in the Bible who stood by himself and whom God thus blessed with spectacular success: Moses, Elijah, Daniel, Jeremiah, Nehemiah, and many others come to mind here. Reflecting on this long line of men who stood alone, we could say it this way: the more alone you are as a man of God, the more likely God is to show up and win the day.

God gave David the victory. This happened throughout much of his kingship. We can only condense what the Lord allowed David to do, but suffice to say that David conquered many enemies, reaped harvests of blessing from the Lord, watched as the people grew in dedication to the Lord, and saw his own house prosper.

The Great Sin of David and the Even Greater Love of God

This all happened despite David's terrible sin with Bathsheba and against Uriah; this sin would eventually tear apart his family and split his kingdom. David was not the true hero of the Bible; this is abundantly clear. Yet even in noting the tragic effects of sin, we cannot fail to see that God blessed David, the man after His own heart (Acts 13:22). David showed that he loved God, in fact, even as the effects of his sin played out.

After David fell and sinned as we all do, he repented. Psalm 51 shows this in spades; it is his prayer following his adultery with Bathsheba, the intentional death of Uriah, and the loss of David's child with Bathsheba. The death of his child seared David like a hot iron. He went before the Lord in humility and confessed his sin directly. His words still speak:

> Have mercy on me, O God,
> according to your steadfast love;
> according to your abundant mercy
> blot out my transgressions.
> Wash me thoroughly from my iniquity,
> and cleanse me from my sin! (Psalm 51:1-2)

David's prayer is a model for us. Every man fails. Every man sins. We must all humble ourselves before God, confess our rebellion, and turn away from it. David hit heights few men have ever hit, but he also hit lows that took him to the edge of despair. Mark this well: God did not burn David up on the spot. As David humbled himself, God forgave him, continued to use him, and loved him.

The story of David is about the boy who became king, yes. But it is even more about the forgiveness and persevering love of God. If God forgave David of his great sin, we may take great encouragement in this: God will forgive *us*, too. As we confess our sin and leave it behind, God will renew, restore, and cleanse us to the full. We will not live with the stain and stench of sin upon us; we will rise, wash our face, and live anew, just as David did (2 Samuel 12:20). We cannot wallow in our shame. When forgiven by God, we must rise and build.

David broke himself to pieces, but God put him back together. This later chapter in David's life teaches us an essential lesson about forgiveness. It is not that we need to forgive ourselves, as we commonly hear today. We are not the judge or ruler of the cosmos; we are not the Creator God. No, we need God's forgiveness. The story of David has great news on this theme: the forgiveness and love of God are not small, as we are tempted to think. He is not a stingy God who offers us only a little thimbleful of forgiveness. God does not roar at us like an angry man drunk with rage to "Get yourself together, you worthless idiot!"

God is not belligerent and unhinged. He is a God of perfect justice, it is true. But God as revealed in Scripture is tender. He is a kind Heavenly Father. He loves to forgive. He delights to save. The forgiveness of God is great forgiveness, pardon to the uttermost. The love of God is great love, without limit or measure. Consider the witness of Lamentations 3:22–23 as testimony to this glorious truth:

The steadfast love of the LORD never ceases;
his mercies never come to an end;
they are new every morning;
great is your faithfulness.

What does this mean, practically? It means this: No man is too far gone for God (nor is any woman). No one can out-sin God's forgiveness. Nor can any Christian—a true believer—lose the love of God. The love of God chose us before the foundation of the world, the love of God sent Christ to the cross to die for our sins, the love of God delivered the gift of saving faith to us through regeneration, and the love of God will keep us safe and secure for all eternity. The love of God does not depend on us; the love of God depends on God.

We'll return to David's story in a moment. But for now, it is worth taking a moment to distinguish our Heavenly Father's love from the love of angry earthly fathers. Sadly, there are many men who have not loved their children well. All of us fail, but some men really do raise their children in a spirit of anger and iron control, with very little love in the equation. So too do mothers fail in these ways. You may be from such a home. Love as you experienced it may have been *conditional*—that is, dependent on your performance and behavior. One minute, you were in the good graces of your parents; the next, you were living under uncontrollable rage.

Or perhaps the home was quieter, but you never measured up to expectations. Love was withheld; it depended on behavior. In some circumstances, legalism dominated, and your childhood was all about rules and regulations, like a neighborhood branch of Big Government. It's not that rules and parental authority are bad, but there was little affection, kindness, and forbearance in your home. If the preceding describes your childhood in some way, you may struggle to love. But more than this: You may also struggle to *be loved*.

Here is what you need if this is true in some form: You need to consider afresh the kind character of our holy God. You need to drink in a love that is not legalistic, conditioned by your performance, or limited. God's love comes with real structure and shape, absolutely. It is not the same as worldly affirmation, where you're not asked to change or repent or alter yourself in any way. No, the love of God bids you come and die to your sin, your selfishness, your past, and your worldly dreams. But once you are born again through repentance, the love of God never runs out.

Your conduct matters greatly to God, and you must strive for holiness by the Spirit's power, never seeking to grieve Him (Ephesians 4:30). The true Christian pursues God zealously. But even when we fail (as we all will, and frequently), God remains faithful to us (2 Timothy 2:13). This is because God's love is bigger, infinitely bigger, than our love. All this we see in David's story; all this speaks not simply to his experience, but to ours.

Conclusion

David sinned greatly against God, as we have seen. But David's story did not end there. The forgiveness of God healed and restored him. God put his feet back on the path, just as He will for us. Years after his epic transgression, when it came time for him to die, David's speech showed that he knew what a man was called to be. Summoning his son Solomon, David said this from his deathbed:

> "I am about to go the way of all the earth. Be strong and show yourself a man." (1 Kings 2:2)

To be a man was to be strong; in being strong, one showed that one was (or is) a man. But where did David urge Solomon to find his strength? In God, and God alone. He urged Solomon to

> "keep the charge of the LORD your God, walking in his ways and keeping his statutes, his commandments, his rules, and his testimonies, as it is written in the Law of Moses, that you may prosper in all that you do and wherever you turn." (v. 3)

This word speaks to us today. Whether or not a father has ever said this to us face-to-face, God says it to us now through His perfect Word. We must not follow our culture. We must not follow our flesh. We must follow Him. We must cry out to Him for help and grace and strength, and then we must live as those who would be strong in the Lord's power. We must not choose sinful, selfish weakness. We cannot stay boys forever.

Praise God, we have hope—infinite hope. Just as God helped and rebuilt David, God will help and rebuild us. We are weak, but God will make us strong. Our culture tells us this is not needed. There is no such thing as manhood, and men who seek to be strong are actually "toxic." But this is a lie. God's Word still speaks, and God's grace still renews. Today, we must indeed "show ourselves a man." We may feel like this is an impossible burden, like we have gone too far, like we have out-sinned God's grace. But none of this is true. Our God is the God of the impossible.

Our God makes all things—all men who turn to Him—new.

CHAPTER 5

The Foundation of Strong Manhood: Jesus Christ

Jesus Christ is a lion in majesty
and a lamb in meekness.

Jonathan Edwards

Our culture tells us that if we live by the flesh, we will be happy. If we embrace our strongest desires and passions, we will become our authentic selves, no longer shackled by the expectations and morals of others. It all sounds good, but living by this antigospel is another matter.

I thought of this truth when I encountered the true testimony of a man I'll call Barabbas. Barabbas lived out the course chartered by the Sexual Revolution. He indulged from a young age in pornography and masturbation; he attended gay pride parades; he developed his bent toward same-sex attraction, and did not counter it.

Barabbas knew what he was doing was wrong. His sin was spreading through him like an incurable disease, but he did not stop it—until he met a woman at church who counseled him with the Gospel and pointed him to one of her pastors, a man named Gavin Peacock, a warm-hearted Christian leader and former soccer star.

Gavin started meeting with Barabbas for biblical counseling and training. In love, he challenged him to attack his sexual sin—not just at the level of behavior, but at the level of heart desire. Where he felt desire for men of the same sex, Gavin urged Barabbas to pray, confess it, turn from it, and ask God for fresh grace to love Christ.

Through all this, God did a miraculous work. Barabbas later said:

> God opened my eyes to see the greatness of salvation in Christ. I knew, at my conversion, that I no longer bore the guilt of past sins. But now I also felt an incredible freedom and courage that came from a clear conscience before God. I have learned about the joy of godly masculinity—the joy of applying all that I am and have in service to Christ and His kingdom. What I lost of my self-made image I have more than gained with the new man He has made me.[1]

Reading an incredible story like this, you cannot help but ask: How can this happen for other men? Having heard endlessly about the "toxicity" of men, is it really possible for a fallen man to change this dramatically?

Here is some very good news: anyone can change. God is in the transformation business. Faith in Jesus is the way we change; following Jesus as our example of godly devotion and biblical manhood is what we most need. In this chapter, we range over the life and ministry of Jesus to understand the one who was truly a strong man for us and our salvation. We discover here that being a strong man of God is not one thing alone. Instead, all who embrace the identity of strong manhood by God's grace must cultivate various traits, take on numerous duties, and at all times strive to emulate Jesus Christ, the strong man *par excellence*.

The Person and Work of Jesus Christ, the True Man

Jesus Christ was and is the true human. He came to Earth as the second Adam. Preexistent before all time with God the Father and God the Spirit, God the Son assumed a human nature alongside His divine nature when He became incarnate. The One who made all things entered the world as a tiny baby, showing us that God did indeed keep His promise to send the "seed" or "offspring" of the woman to rescue His people (see Genesis 3:15). When God appointed and delivered a warrior-redeemer, He did so not by dispatching an army of 100,000 angels, but by giving a young virgin woman conception by the Holy Spirit (Luke 1:35). The greater David came into this world not by thundering from on high, but through the normal process of birth. Jesus was a boy when He came into the world, and He soon grew into a man.

It is important that we square with this reality right off the bat. The evangelical church of our day struggles to understand the manliness of Jesus, so we need to say a few words here. Jesus is, of course, the example for every believer, regardless of their gender. Not only men can learn from His life, teaching, and ministry; every Christian can, should, and must. But having noted this, we must also hasten to add that Jesus was not androgynous. He was and is male. His masculinity does not close Him off from women seeking to be like Him. The gospels of the New Testament show us that women flocked to Jesus and loved Him dearly. But nonetheless, Jesus still models manhood for men. He shows them the peak and epitome of it. He gives us both an example to follow and the saving power to do so.

Jesus, we see first, communed with God. If we spend a good amount of time among men who still believe in being masculine, whether they are Christian or not, we might sense from them an ambivalence to spirituality. Manly men, the idea sometimes goes, like practical realities. We don't give much attention to fluffy pieties; we leave that to women. Women sit around and pray and study the Bible, while men do stuff, build stuff, and fix stuff.

In reality, nothing could be further from the truth. The true man Jesus Christ loved God. He was hungry for God's Word. When He was just a boy, His parents found Him in the Temple. While there, He sat among the Jewish teachers, "listening to them and asking them questions" (Luke 2:46). He had great spiritual curiosity. He also had great insight: "all who heard him were amazed at his understanding and his answers" (Luke 2:47). Jesus had unbroken interest in the things of God. He wanted to draw near to His heavenly Father. As time went on, He "increased in wisdom and in stature and in favor with God and man" (Luke 2:52).

This tells us much about boys. Obviously, no son of ours will have a divine nature! We cannot expect perfection of our boys or ourselves, and must in fact studiously guard against—and repent of—such expectations. Having noted this, though, Jesus shows us that it is not off-putting for a boy to pursue the knowledge and love of God. This is in fact what boys most need—more than they need anything else. They need God. They need communion with God. They need to learn the truth of God. They need to sit at the feet of the Word of God. Manhood is more than communion with God through prayer and Bible learning, but we must mark this well: it is never less than this. In fact, there will be no true manhood without it (and without the atonement, as we shall explore below).

Men must never be ashamed of prayer, Bible study, meditation, and loving church. When I was a boy, my classmates mocked me for being a Christian. Once a traveling basketball troupe came to my town in Maine. It was not quite the Harlem Globetrotters; it was like a B-list version of them. Still, it was heady stuff for my small town, and I attended their nighttime game against the local college team. They asked us all to pray, and I bowed my head. As I raised my head, I saw two boys from my class pointing at me and laughing. They shamed me for being a Christian.

I can still feel the hot wave of embarrassment wash over me; I felt like such an idiot compared to them in their coolness. Yet God used that moment in my life: He taught me then, and many times since, that masculine "coolness" does nothing for my eternal soul. What matters is not looking good or being above it all. What matters is this: God working in us so that we draw near to Him in the humility of repentance.

Jesus's Devotion to God

Though no sinner like you and I, Jesus made time for fellowship with God. He was the Son of God, yet He knew that He Himself needed to be alone with His Father. We read of His devotion in Mark 1:35, which tells us about His habits early in the day: "And rising very early in the morning, while it was still dark, he departed and went out to a desolate place, and there he prayed." We need to emulate Jesus. We should do so not in an effort to earn our salvation or convince God to give us what we want. We should pray because God loves us, has saved us, and has called us to Himself. If Jesus had such instincts, so should every man.

Jesus was utterly devoted to God—as a boy, as a young man, and as an adult. We do not have much material at all on His years before going into ministry when He was about thirty. The Bible veils them in the perfect wisdom of God. What we do discover in Matthew's gospel is that when Jesus began His earthly ministry, it was like being shot out of a cannon. He was a man abandoned to the Lord—utterly devoted, totally consecrated, zero percent worried about what others thought, and zealous for His Father's glory.

Jesus got a great opportunity to demonstrate this right as His ministry began. The Spirit led him into the wilderness for one express purpose: "to be tempted by the devil" (Matthew 4:1). Incredibly, Jesus fasted for forty days and nights before facing this temptation. He shows us how we should handle the lies of the devil when they are presented to us, whether we feel weak or strong.

Jesus entered that battle of His ongoing war with the serpent as the "tempter" tried to entice him three different times to follow his wicked ways. First, the devil played on Jesus's hunger from fasting. "If you are the Son of God," Satan declared, "command these stones to become loaves of bread" (Matthew 4:3). Just as he had lured Adam into rebellion through food, so Satan tried to use Jesus's knee-buckling hunger the same way. Jesus had greater provision before Him, though. He cited Deuteronomy 8:3 to ward off the devil: "It is written, 'Man shall not live by bread alone, but by every word that comes from the mouth of God'" (Matthew 4:4).

Next, Satan took Jesus to Jerusalem, placing him "on the pinnacle of the temple" (Matthew 4:5). This was a strategic location. At the site ostensibly dedicated to the worship of God, Satan tried to get Jesus to embrace the folly of fleshliness. He urged Him to jump off the Temple's peak, saying the angels would bear Him up per Psalm 91:11–12. Satan revealed here that he knew (and knows) something of the Word of God, and that it is his business and pleasure to twist it for his wicked purposes. In truth, Satan wanted Jesus to do what Satan did: test the Lord. Go against Him. Misuse what God had given Him. But Jesus cited Isaiah 7:12: "Again it is written, 'You shall not put the Lord your God to the test'" (Matthew 4:7). Where Satan thrashed against God's will, trying to best it, Jesus submitted Himself to God's will, loving it and receiving it for His own good. True manhood does not mean looking cool while you go your own way; true manhood looks like submitting to God as Jesus did.

After this, Satan tried one more time, throwing everything he had at Jesus. He took Him to the mountaintop "and showed him all the kingdoms of the world and their glory" (Matthew 4:8). He told Him he would give the Son of God all this if He would "fall down and worship" (v. 9). A more brazen temptation has never traveled through soundwaves than this. The devil did not ultimately own the kingdoms he showed Christ. Yes, he had and has fearsome power in this realm, that is true. But this is like a man who dresses up as the British prime minister calling the actual prime minister into his home office and telling him, "I'll give you the keys to the British navy if you just recognize my authority."

Yes, the devil operates as the "ruler" of this world, as Christ Himself said. But Jesus had come to Earth to bind the devil and overcome the effects of his diabolical reign (Matthew 12:29–30). As He said in John's gospel: "Now is the judgment of this world; now will the ruler of this world be cast out" (John 12:31). Jesus was not hoping to do this; Jesus did this by His atoning death and life-giving resurrection.

Back to the scene of temptation. It all came down to this: Would Jesus worship the true God, or Satan? Tragically, when facing this same choice, many around us make the wrong choice here. They follow their flesh, their sin, and their natural instincts. Satan, in turn, gives them what their heart desires, just so long as they worship him and do nothing to disrupt his diabolical doings. But Jesus shows us how a true man chooses in this contest of worship. Citing Deuteronomy 6:13, He rallied all His strength and thundered back, "Be gone, Satan! For it is written, 'You shall worship the Lord your God, and him only shall you serve.'" What a rebuke this is; what a manly response, driven by a three-word command!

As I have noted, the devil possesses a great measure of agency for evil. But he probably could not reply when so drenched in the power of Christ's holy rebuke. The text tells us: "Then the devil left him, and behold, angels came and were ministering to him" (Matthew 4:11). Thus ended the first official battle between the serpent and the seed of the woman. The Son of God won it, and the devil could only slink away. But the Son of God did not defeat His foe on that day by using His omnipotent might to vaporize Satan; He won by knowing the Word, trusting in it, and standing on it. In so doing, Jesus shows us how godly men must live. We know that we will face our own temptations, and so we must be armed with God's truth to defeat the devil's lies.

We do not live in peacetime. There is a violent clash between Heaven and Hell going on all around us at every moment. This world truly is the site of the war between God's forces and Satan's forces. It is not that we *could* find ourselves in this fight; it is that every single human being, and all creation besides, *is* in this fight. The only question before us is this: whose side will we join? Which ruler will we serve—the heavenly one or the hellish one? By putting this devotion on display in the wilderness temptations, Jesus shows us the way.

We are not made to give in to temptation; we are made to engage it and overcome it. A strong man rejects the way of the evil one, Satan, and depends on God for all his strength. In so doing, he emulates his Savior and passes the test—which he must do over and over again in this life.[2]

Jesus, Both Tough and Tender

Third, Jesus was both tough and tender while incarnate, in order to die sacrificially. Jesus was not tough *or* tender; He displayed both of them truly. Before we think extendedly about His kindness, let's think about His toughness.

When He saw that merchants in the Temple had no care for God's holiness but only their own profits, Jesus wove a whip out of cords and scourged the moneychangers and profiteers. On that day, Jesus showed righteous anger over blasphemy. He took reverence for God's holiness personally.

Nor did Jesus shy away from tough speech. When Peter urged Him to believe that He did not need to die for sinners, Jesus rebuked him in the severest terms: "Get behind me, Satan," He roared (Matthew 16:23).

As we can see, Jesus was not scared to speak strongly, act with conviction, or defy evil unflinchingly. The Son of God was not easy to knock off course; in fact, He could not be knocked off course. Once the end of His life came in sight, He set His face like flint. He resolved to go to Jerusalem to die for the godless, and nothing turned Him aside from that fate (Luke 9:51).

Here was manliness in divine form. Jesus did not cast about without a plan; He got His marching orders from His Father, He busied himself with His Father's business, and He never turned away from the purpose before Him.

This is instructive for us men. It is not always easy for us to get a plan. Further, Jesus had a much more defined plan than we can imagine—we will never have to save sinners by dying on a cross under sentence of God's wrath! Only He could do this. But like Jesus, we will thrive when we live on mission, when we figure out what we are best at, and when we put all our energy into tackling just that kind of grand strategy.

Jesus was ridiculously focused. He was single-minded. Because He loved His Father's name and reputation, He brooked no compromise with evil or weakness. He gives us men a shining portrait of toughness, and we must pray that we emulate Him. We too must resolve to carry our cross; every Christian must, and we men must lead out in this labor of love (Luke 9:23). All this mission focus rebukes our passive, fearful, and effeminate culture, which encourages us to be timid men. Such a man does not have a plan; he does not live on mission; he is not in what soldiers call a forward position—one that is charged and ready for battle. Instead, he lives on his heels. He does not act with initiative; he lives passively and fearfully, afraid to take a risk or set a course because it might be the wrong one.

Jesus shows us a better way than this. There are many moments when we will be confused. Further, we will sin, err, and stumble, unlike our Savior (James 3:2). But men cannot embrace softness. We must embrace resolution and an appropriate toughness. By nature, we are all angry men, for we all sin. Beyond this, many of us have a tendency toward softness, toward passivity, toward hopelessness and aimlessness (especially in a safety-driven, anti-masculine culture like ours). But Jesus points His finger and shows us the way out. We cannot do our own work perfectly as He did, but we can surely emulate Him in His zeal for God's Kingdom and purposes. When we do the same, we will find tremendous meaning and joy.

The work Jesus took up called for immense toughness. But it was tender work as well. It was grounded in the love of God and love for the wicked. Jesus loved His Father, and so His own earthly activity was powered, every second, by that affection and His desire to please God (and by the indwelling Holy Spirit).[3] At the same time, Jesus came to Earth for the express duty of laying down His life for sinners. His death on the cross would satisfy the Father's just wrath against sin and cleanse the guilty of all their wickedness. So even as Jesus operated all the time out of love for the Father, so too did He order His mind and heart around the great work of redemption. The work that called for so much toughness came from a place of great tenderness.

Even before the cross, we see how Jesus treated others kindly and gently. His whole ministry was marked by liberation, healing, and transformation. Everywhere Jesus went, blessing followed. He did not keep Himself above the people, lording His heavenly magnificence over everyone around Him. Yes, Jesus showed His authority repeatedly and did not shy away from such demonstrations. But He exhibited a gracious and controlled spirit all throughout the gospels—one that we men must learn from if we would be strong men of the Christlike kind.[4]

Jesus, Kind and Gentle

Jesus was greatly concerned about people. He treated them as what they were and are: image-bearers of God. Jesus exercised a healing ministry that put people back together again, and He did so in a day when there was no expert medical care of the kind we take for granted. For example, when Peter's mother-in-law lay sick, "He touched her hand, and the fever left her, and she rose and began to serve him" (Matthew 8:15). Healing begat more healing. People could not stay away from the kind miracle worker:

> That evening they brought to him many who were oppressed by demons, and he cast out the spirits with a word and healed all who were sick. This was to fulfill what was spoken by the prophet Isaiah: "He took our illnesses and bore our diseases." (vv. 16–17)

The Son of God came to Earth not to be lauded, but to love.

Jesus not only cared for adults, but children. They did not bother Him; He welcomed them into His presence. We see this kindness in action in Matthew 19:13–15, where His disciples actually go so far as to try to keep boys and girls away from Jesus. His response tells us much about His heart:

> Then children were brought to him that he might lay his hands on them and pray. The disciples rebuked the people, but Jesus said, "Let the little children come to me and do not hinder them, for to such belongs the kingdom of heaven." And he laid his hands on them and went away.

The people around Jesus wanted Him to pray for their children. Instead of being bothered by this, Jesus shows us the higher way, the way of love. He welcomed the children to Him. In doing so, He gives us men a picture of how we should engage boys and girls. It can be easy for us to be distracted and even bothered by our children, but we must welcome them, treasure them, and treat them with real kindness.

In this episode, as in others, Jesus enfleshes what He says in Matthew 11:28–29: He invited "all who labor and are heavy laden" to come to Him so that He could give them rest (v. 28). We can scarcely find a more encouraging word than this in all the Bible. Jesus does not refuse all but the best behaved and most proficient. He is not a Savior for those who have all their act together and every detail of their life buttoned up. No, Jesus invites the needy to His side. Jesus beckons the helpless forward. Jesus knows they will drain His energy, take His time, and exhaust His finite human strength, but He does not refuse them. He came to give rest—the rest of salvation—and His heart is generous.

Indeed, Jesus described that heart here. He says He is "gentle and lowly in heart," a marvelous summation of His character (v. 29). We remember on this count the character of the Old Testament leader

Moses. As Numbers 12:3 records, "Now the man Moses was very meek, more than all people who were on the face of the earth." Both Moses and Jesus both had the ability to ramp up and call out evil in no uncertain terms, but we cannot fail to see that Moses was described by God's own Word as "very meek," a man who did not hold himself imperiously above others. Quite the opposite: Moses's closeness to God meant he carried himself in a lowly manner.

This was all just a shadow of the character of the greater Moses, the God-man. Moses had to fight indwelling sin, after all, and failed repeatedly in his calling. But Jesus never failed. Jesus never sinned. Jesus never doubted God. Jesus never came within a thousand miles of sin. Further, while Moses was indeed meek, Jesus was the epitome of meekness and gentleness. His whole life was power under restraint. Jesus lived in humility. He served His disciples, the sick, the needy, the lowly, and the undeserving. Jesus is a model for us, much as we will all fail to meet His standard.

Jesus, Servant of All

Jesus Christ is the most wondrous person there is, was, or will be. Jesus was and is the God of all the earth, the One who created the earth and sustains all things in existence. Yet as a man, Jesus's life was very simple, even a poor man's life. His days were clear of all thirst for worldly renown, for His entire purpose was to serve others.

We get a final glimpse of such godly character just before He goes to the cross. After eating His final meal with His disciples, Jesus

> laid aside his outer garments, and taking a towel, tied it around his waist. Then he poured water into a basin and began to wash the disciples' feet and to wipe them with the towel that was wrapped around him. (John 13:4–5)

This was a task of the most profound humility, one reserved for the least important servant or slave in a household. Yet this is what Jesus gladly did for His beloved disciples, for two reasons. The first was to display the attitude of a true follower of Christ. Jesus said this explicitly: "I have given you an example, that you also should do just as I have done to you" (v. 15). Jesus was not *only* showing His disciples rich and undeserved kindness; He was enfleshing the entire nature of Christianity. Christians do not exalt themselves. Sinners naturally do, but people regenerated by the Spirit humble themselves. Accordingly, this is what men of God do.

The true man, Jesus Christ, got down on His hands and knees and performed basically the lowest task an ancient person could. There is no limit to our servanthood, Jesus taught us then. We men must not hang back and let others model this, either; we must be first in serving others. I do not mean by saying this that we practice "servant leadership" as some understand it. Jesus served His disciples as we are seeing, but He led His charges. He made decisions, exercised authority, and was the head of the movement He started. There need not be any tension, then, between having the mindset of a humble servant and acting as the leader in a given context.

Jesus was not only modeling the demeanor of a true disciple, however. In washing the disciples' feet, secondly, Jesus was giving them a sense of what they needed spiritually. Their greatest need was to be clean in their soul, not simply their feet (v. 10). This was why Jesus was headed to the cross: He was going to take their sin on Himself, drink the Father's just wrath against that sin, wash them completely clean of all guilt and shame, and die. Jesus died in agony and humiliation on the cross so that we could experience the neverending love and forgiveness of the Father. Jesus lived for others, not Himself. In the same way, Jesus died for others, not Himself.

Jesus died as *both* a servant and a warrior.[5] Stated another way, on the cross, Jesus served as both lamb and lion. His crucifixion put both roles on display. In dying, Jesus laid down His life as a sacrificial offering for His people. He served us by dying for us. He did not fight the Jewish or Roman authorities that played a role in His taking a criminal's place on a cruel cross; He willingly suffered tremendous pain and indignity to atone for all the sins of His people. Jesus was the Lamb of God, and His sacrifice was perfectly sufficient for all our sin; through His death, we know total forgiveness when we repent and trust Him as our Savior and Lord.

In His death, Jesus also acted as the warrior-savior. He came in order to "destroy the works of the devil" (1 John 3:8). When He died, Jesus played the role of the conqueror, for His atonement for our sin released us from the devil's power. The devil holds in his sway all whose sins accuse them due to lack of atonement; he terrorizes them with the specter of death, drenching them in fear. But when Jesus died, He freed all His people from the power of sin, and thereby freed us from the power of death. We no longer have to fear death because Christ died for us.

So we see that Jesus came as the strong man for us. He came to fight for us, but His campaign against Satan looked different than many expected it would. In His first coming, Jesus did not battle Satan by hurling lightning bolts at him. He battled Satan by washing all our sins away and taking us out of the clutches of the serpent himself. Doing so required Him to lay down His life, take our place, bear our sin, and bear the Father's just wrath that we deserved to experience. Because Jesus died in our stead, we are free. The warrior, we see, is the servant; the servant is the warrior. The lion is the lamb; the lamb is the lion. Because of Christ, all our sin is atoned for, and we have peace with God and the certain hope of eternal life in the new heaven and new earth.

Christ's humility should stagger us. Even as God saves and grows us, we should never stop pursuing Christlikeness. Though the very Son of God, Jesus stooped to save us. In His death, we see how far our love for others is to go and the degree of humility that must characterize us. By the grace of God working in us, we are to pursue at all times a humble and lowly mindset. The Apostle Paul told the entire church in Philippi, "Have this mind among yourselves," a mind that led to Christ "taking the form of a servant, being born in the likeness of men," and meaning that Christ "humbled himself by becoming obedient to the point of death, even death on a cross" (Philippians 2:5–8).

Leaders of a worldly stripe lord their authority *over* others. But leaders of a Christlike stripe lay down their lives *for* others. As men called to lead in certain ways (as the next chapter explores), we must continually remember and pray for a heart drenched in humility like Christ's. Our world exalts high and mighty leaders, but God exalts humble and meek servants. This is the kind of man God blesses; this is the kind of man we should pray to become.

Conclusion

Reading this chapter may leave you thinking, "How on earth can I, who struggles with sin, be like Jesus Christ, the true Man?" That is a great question! Strong, godly manhood, as we have seen, is not reduced to one quality alone. Like Christ himself, a strong man of God must be many-sided and multidimensional. He can only live in such a way if God works in his heart and supplies the grace for such godliness, as He does and will do for all of us imperfect and naturally weak men.

This is how a man like Barabbas crosses over from living death to eternal life. This is how you and I, sinners all, can both know Christ as our Savior and live for Him daily following our conversion. The power for such godliness is not found in us; it is all found in Christ, and He will not withhold it. We could say it this way: Jesus Christ is the *model*, even as He is the *means* by which we grow. In Him, we see that biblical manhood is not one thing alone; biblical manhood is many things. It involves numerous traits, duties, and affections. Through Christ, we can live it out to the glory of our Redeemer.

CHAPTER 6

The Foundation of Strong Manhood: New Testament Teaching

It has been said that as goes the family, so goes the world. It can also be said that as goes the father, so goes the family.

Voddie Baucham Jr.

The situation is a common one in these confused days. A young couple trying to sort out roles in the home: the man, frustrated; the woman, not a little concerned by his temper. What are the circumstances of this troubled situation? Alongside the normal sins and challenges of marriage, he stays at home, caring for the baby while she draws a higher salary and thus functions as the provider of the family.

I first encountered this scenario in a Tide commercial over a decade ago. A man cheerfully bounced around his sun-strewn suburban home, chirping at the camera while folding a buoyant batch of laundry. Not only this, but he went so far as to declare himself a "dad-mom" in the ad. Though I was quite familiar with the long march of feminism and its many ill effects, I had never heard this term. Little did I know it would catch on in serious measure in the years to follow.

For purposes of clarity, let's update Tide's language. Let's call this phenomenon the "Mr. Mom" identity. Our culture teaches us that men can freely and happily take on this role—women can be the provider of the family, and men can be the homemaker and primary childraiser. But this is not the biblical model. Men should surely engage their children and home in all sorts of ways; men should be loving, compassionate, kind, and approachable. But this does not obscure a central truth: men are not made to be Mr. Mom. Nor are they called to this role in ordinary terms.

Men may face unemployment or disability and have to take on duties they would not otherwise perform. But outside of such exceptions, asking men to be Mr. Mom is a recipe for disaster. It will either breed complacent happiness in a setting that is not a man's to own, or it will more often produce frustration and unresolved tension as he embraces a purpose to which God has not called him. Few will say this today, I know; in our gender-neutral order, in fact, men are openly encouraged to be feminine and women are openly encouraged to be masculine. The biblical pattern is reversed, and few speak up about this. To go against nature is now second nature.

In such disordered days, we need the clarifying truths of God's Word. Men need to hear from God how they are designed and constituted. In this chapter, we study how the man claimed by Christ should live and act and think. We will first consider the distinctiveness of the sexes, as controversial a reality in the New Testament age as in ours. We will then study several important teachings about the man's given role per the call of God: husband, father, provider, head, laborer, churchman, elder, single man. This material will relieve confusion and resolve frustration, much as we all must fight sin daily. Many men around us are tragically misdirected, but the man of God has the great privilege of living according to the nature given him by his Maker and Redeemer.

The Distinctiveness of the Sexes in Romans 1

Our biblical foundation introduced us to the central idea that our culture hates passionately today: God has made us either a man or a woman for His glory. That is all there is in terms of "gender identity": two sexes. Men and women. There is no in-between, there is no third category, and there is no option to make one's own identity. Our calling as image-bearers is not to create our self-conception, but to receive our bodies as a gift from God. Per God's instruction, our body and our identity are one. Those born into a male body are men; those born into a female body are women.

Aside from the reality that God is the Creator of all, our neo-pagan culture despises nothing more than what we have just said. It is true: reality itself is controversial today. Stating the basic truths plunges us into a frenzy of name-calling and motive-judging. A public square listening to the hiss of the serpent rather than the Voice from the heavens despises the sexes and the order of creation. Yet Christians have no option of conforming to the world's "wisdom," which is no wisdom at all. We can only stand upon God's truth, stand for it, and stand behind it as Satan does his worst to defy it.

We have no choice before us but to speak the truth, come what may. Based on the Word of God, the sexes are distinct. There is an order that flows from this, and there is natural behavior and a natural way of life that gives God glory as we live according to His design. Conversely, there is also deeply unnatural behavior and ideology, which Paul discusses in Romans 1:18–27, an ancient passage that speaks to our modern chaos. In this stunning section of Scripture, Paul maps out what paganism—the anti-Creator worldview that urges us to live according to our fleshly desires—delivers.

This philosophy that recurs across all human history is based, quite simply, in thanklessness. Writing of unbelievers, Paul says this:

> For although they knew God, they did not honor him as God or give thanks to him, but they became futile in their thinking, and their foolish hearts were darkened. (Romans 1:21)

Humanity naturally lives a thankless existence. We enjoy many common-grace blessings from God, but do not give Him glory or thanks. Instead, we suppress our awareness of His kindness and pretend He does not exist. In our flesh, we do not have an *information problem*, as if we just needed the right arguments to prove that God is real. We have a *suppression problem*, for we know the Creator lives but hate this truth, and so adopt a mindset that suppresses it (and the gratefulness it should draw out).

Because of this, God gives people over to impure lusts, to sexual brazenness (vv. 24–25). Not only this, but He gives people over to "dishonorable passions" so that we practice pagan sexuality of various kinds, including homosexuality (vv. 26–27). Such wickedness is against God's moral will and also "contrary to nature" (v. 26). The Greek term Paul uses here, *phusin*, reveals that God has written what is natural and what is unnatural onto our conscience. Scripture is essential to us, but our inborn understanding of humanity and morality given to us by God also witnesses to us. There is an order of "nature" that God set up that we all comprehend even without instruction and that we violate at our great peril. This order is based on the unchangeable realities of manhood, womanhood, and

God-designed sexuality, each of which is ordered to the God-given institution of marriage.

The Distinctiveness of the Sexes in 1 Corinthians 11

Paul expanded upon "nature" and the order of creation in 1 Corinthians 11:2–16. It is very significant that he did so to the Corinthian church, for they, like the Christians in Rome, were surrounded by pagan sexuality. Androgyny was everywhere. If anything, in fact, the church at Corinth faced *greater* pressure to conform to a fallen gender order than we do. Corinth not only featured sexual libertinism on an epic scale, but

> was a major centre of the Dionysian cult, a religion where male adherents would don feminine apparel in imitation of the god himself, who was closely associated with feminine clothing—the other name by which he is known, Bacchus, is derived from the word *bassara*, a woman's dress.[1]

Along these lines, the Corinthians did not blush at temple prostitution. In terms that resonate with our age, they celebrated it. Sexual depravity of an upside-down kind was rampant in this port city, where sailors and visitors the world over went to "blow off steam." If we feel like paganism is everywhere around us today, we may take (ironic) encouragement in this: such a sense is not a modern experience, but an ancient one.

Instead of going silent about creational realities and focusing only on expressly "spiritual" matters, Paul took pains to detail for the Corinthians the God-ordained distinctiveness of the sexes. First, he wrote, the Church should follow the order established by God: "But I want you to understand that the head of every man is Christ, the head of a wife is her husband, and the head of Christ is God" (v. 3).

The passage is complex and takes some twists and turns, but suffice to say that this order is displayed through the distinctive physical appearance of men and women. Specifically, a woman should show that she is under her husband's authority by keeping her hair long and thus covering her head. Some in Corinth would have scoffed at such an idea, but Paul did not back down:

> For a man ought not to cover his head, since he is the image
> and glory of God, but woman is the glory of man. For
> man was not made from woman, but woman from man.
> Neither was man created for woman, but woman for man.
> (vv. 7–10)

Paul then concludes:

> Does not nature itself teach you that if a man wears long
> hair it is a disgrace for him, but if a woman has long hair,
> it is her glory? For her hair is given to her for a covering.
> (vv. 14–15)

Here is a vital truth for understanding manhood, womanhood, and humanity most broadly. As we saw in Romans 1, Paul teaches that there is a reality called "nature." It is constituted and defined by God, not man. With all due apologies to the man-bun, there is something about a man having long hair that everyone can see is *atimia*, a "disgrace" in the Greek. Conversely, a woman who has long hair is covered—quite literally—in *chabod*, "glory." She is to be covered in this way as a sign of her submission to her husband. He is not to be covered by long hair; doing so drapes him in the sign God has given to women, not men.

Androgyny is no new idea. It is an ancient problem. It preyed upon the Corinthians about two thousand years ago just as it preys upon us. Androgyny is profoundly dishonoring to God. There surely are gray areas of appearance and dress among the sexes; both may wear pants, both may wear T-shirts, both worship God through Christ, and on we could go. But at their base, God has made men and women to look distinctive and to act distinctly. The order of creation matters. The man was made first and given "authority" in his home by God. He is his wife's "head." He is called to love her lavishly, and she is called to submit to him joyfully.

But Paul does not confine his teaching on the sexes to spiritual truths, massively important as they are. He goes further; he leaves no room for Gnostic Christianity where the soul matters and the body does not. No, he teaches that across cultures, men should look like men and women should look like women. This is not "legalism," as we sometimes hear. Nor is it hairsplitting (no pun intended). Without getting lost in the weeds, the principle Paul teaches the Corinthian church is this: dressing, looking, and acting like a man (or a woman) is a matter of obedience to God and the honoring of God-designed nature. The distinctiveness of the sexes is a matter of God's glory. For our purposes, embodied manhood, looking and acting like a man, is living doxology.

The High Calling of the Christian Husband

Paul not only laid out the distinctiveness of men and women; he gave us the world's most beautiful passage on the meaning of marriage, which is based on the "twoness" of manhood and womanhood. Marriage is not whatever we choose to make it, as our culture tells us.

Marriage is one man uniting with one woman in a lifelong covenant. Marriage is thus a living enfleshment of the Gospel, portraying the relationship between Christ and His blood-bought Church. All this forms our understanding of the husband's role. Speaking to the form Christian marriage should take, Paul tells husbands this:

> Husbands, love your wives, as Christ loved the church and gave himself up for her, that he might sanctify her, having cleansed her by the washing of water with the word, so that he might present the church to himself in splendor, without spot or wrinkle or any such thing, that she might be holy and without blemish. In the same way husbands should love their wives as their own bodies. He who loves his wife loves himself. For no one ever hated his own flesh, but nourishes and cherishes it, just as Christ does the church, because we are members of his body. (Ephesians 5:25–30)

What an incredibly high standard this is! We men are called to love our wives to the fullest extent—in fact, we are called to love them in the imprint of Christ. This is no accommodated conception of marriage where we clear a low bar, do some basic duties, and then chase our own pursuits. This is an enchanted conception of marriage. It promises to take everything we have—and then some.

Our burden for our wife is first spiritual. This is far more important to us as Christian men than how she looks, how people perceive her, or what she does for our reputation as men. We love our wife as a fellow Christian. We want her to flourish as a believer. We are men who seek the holiness of our wife, which means that we are called to provide spiritual help to her, not leaving her to herself. All around us, men will prioritize anything but their wife's spiritual state. They will allow themselves to be distracted by lesser things. In some cases, they will think so little of their wife that they allow their hearts to drift toward another woman. We must always remember that this is not "falling in love" in an excusable and even unchosen way; love is always a choice, not an involuntary force.

In the same way, marriage is not an unending state of bliss, as the movies sometimes portray it. Marriage is a daily commitment. Fidelity is a muscle that we must exercise every single day of our lives. It is fundamentally other-directed. Our love for our wife should be equivalent to our own natural, in-built love for ourselves (v. 28). Our love is not a mere principle, but practical, nourishing, and cherishing (v. 29). It is love that leads our wives to the refreshment of the "water" of the Word (v. 27). We are not the sanctifiers of our wives; that is the Spirit's role. But we do seek in practical ways to encourage our wives with biblical truth, reading Scripture with them, praying with them, talking about theological matters with them, and generally leading them as men of God.

Again, our standard here is none other than Christ Himself. This could not be a higher call. It could not more challenge our innate selfishness. As we read over a passage like Ephesians 5, it will not be hard for us to be convicted by it. We will all see ways in which we fail to meet the divine standard of Jesus. Thankfully God knows this, operates by this, and loves to forgive and bless and renew. We are not now the man we should be, but God will not abandon us. He will keep working on us and growing us until the day we die. His standard is high, very high—but it is matched by the depth of grace that He gives to His children.

All that we need, we have. According to Peter, we need to live *understandingly* with our wives. Peter and Paul thus speak with one voice to us. They set out the high calling of Christian husbands. In 1 Peter 3:7, we read this about our duty:

> Likewise, husbands, live with your wives in an under-
> standing way, showing honor to the woman as the weaker
> vessel, since they are heirs with you of the grace of life, so
> that your prayers may not be hindered.

Strong men of God must be understanding, compassionate, and kind men. Those given a wife by God have a call to understand both the nature of biblical womanhood and the unique identity of their own spouse. They must not think of their wife as a female "buddy." Instead, she is the "weaker vessel," akin to fine china that must be handled carefully and tenderly. She is a precious gift of God, and God Himself watches husbands as they care for the ones He's given them. She is no common household item, but rather deserves great "honor" as a woman of God. Peter's words remind us that it is not "simping" to love your wife, care for her, ask her what she needs of you, and adjust your family life to bless and strengthen her in every way you can. It is godliness in action—and it is manliness displayed.

Treasuring Your Wife and Children

Not long ago, I heard the funniest prayer request I've yet encoun-tered: a godly young man asking for prayer to "understand women." Every time I think about that request, I crack up. But the truth is, all men need help here. Scripture shows us that men do indeed have to work to understand their wives. Though members of the one human race, both made in the image of God, men and women are different from one another in some key ways. To love a woman well, a man must strive to understand her. He will find himself challenged by this at times, and even when he is depending on the grace of God to empower his godly husbanding, he will still hit limits. He will not ever be able to *be Christ* to his wife; she is a sinner in equal need of His saving mercy, and so will bring her own challenges to the relationship. Even when the man strives to comprehend her moods and whims and desires, he will find himself perplexed in some instances.

At this point, we should feel free to be honest: There is a certain strangeness to marriage that we must not miss or try to erase. God did not unite men and men in marriage, or women and women. As Jesus taught in Matthew 19:3-6 (based on Genesis 2), God put together one man and one woman, and He did so having made them distinct from one another, with different instincts, different interests, different needs, and different bodies. This differentness can cause real frustrations. It surely does. But much as we need to navigate our differences well, we also need to remember this: it is in our differences that we discover a sense of wonder.

We should not be thrown off by wonder. In a scientistic age that reduces the glories of the cosmos to atheistic formulations, we will be tempted to look askance at wonder. We do not want to marvel at anything anymore; we want to master the cosmos and use it for our own ends. But there is a very healthy place in the biblical worldview for wonder, and it is birthed when we perceive differences from us. God is wonder to us, for God is Creator and we are not. But wonder is not only found in the contemplation of God; wonder abounds in marriage.

What do I mean? A husband works hard to know and love his wife, but even when he does so over months and years and decades, she is still her own unique person, and she still surprises him, and—it must be said—at times she baffles him. But this is not necessarily bad or evil. A wife is beautiful to her husband; with her different frame and different makeup, she stands apart from him, and he treasures her. In maturity, he loves her distinctiveness; most of the time, he does not fight it or resent it. It is not a threat to him; it is a joy to him.

Distinctiveness never goes away. Even when a couple deeply loves one another and lives out the Gospel paradigm for marriage—Christ laying down His life for the Church, the Church joyfully submitting to Christ—the two spouses grow close but never become the same. For a man's part, the uniqueness of his wife evokes love and delight and care in him. She helps him immeasurably, and he treasures her unboundedly.

It is not all Hallmark cards and roses, though. Sin happens in a marriage. One's earthly spouse is not and cannot be Christ. When the couple does fight and get wounded and even end up in some challenging patterns, they go back to the Lord in repentance, and the Lord forgives them and heals them. The journey continues, and the wonder keeps coming. It is not a quick fling that a godly man yearns for; it is a seven-decade marriage that he longs to have.

Over all those years, by the kindness of God, a godly man's love for his wife never dries up. As the decades go on, time does not shrivel up the marriage; time deepens the bond of love that has long existed, like roots growing inches at a time that give a tree a foundation stronger than cement. This is why marriage is not meant for a year or five years; it is meant, normally, for a lifetime, for the best of it is only experienced as maturity sets in and character proves itself.[2]

By God's grace, men must exercise the same sort of thoughtful and tender approach with their children. The New Testament does not say a great deal about the precise shape of fatherhood, but Colossians 3:21 warns us against exasperating our children: "Fathers, do not provoke your children, lest they become discouraged." This helps us understand ourselves, at least in terms of a general tendency. Fathers can be hard; fathers can be unyielding; fathers can have standards that no child can meet. This is an unbiblical and ungodly situation.

We all stumble as fathers; we all must grow in patience and love toward our children. Praise God, by the power of Christ in us, we can treasure our children, not provoke them. This happens when we give significant time to them, walking through life with them, turning down opportunities we could have taken in order to be with them, laughing with them, playing with them, meeting them where they are. Even where we have faltered in past days in these respects, we can know that God's grace will help and heal what is weak.

We men can fail on either side of the spectrum. We can be too soft and not train our children in the grace of obedience, or we can be too hard and not show gentleness and kindness to our children. Neither approach represents actual Christian love. Our calling is to study Scripture, know our own weaknesses in light of biblical fatherhood, and pray to God for transformation and growth where we must change. Our goal in all this is not merely to raise sons and daughters as God blesses; our goal is to glorify God by enjoying and loving our children and discipling them in the Christian faith.

In all this, the person and work of Christ forms our focus. We cannot save our wife or our kids. God has not asked us to do this. While we have real and serious duties, we must leave our loved ones to God. We should do so in a spirit of trust, hope, confidence, and calmness. We cannot atone for sin—ours or anyone else's. But Jesus can, Jesus has, and Jesus will never leave us nor forsake us. Further, God is the One who works in people to make them "will and do of his good pleasure" (Philippians 2:13), not us. Remembering this will relieve discouragement, ease pressure, relax us, and help us love well.

Jesus is our focus, not us. We are not the ideal spouse, after all; Jesus is the true Husband and is married for all eternity to His people, the Church. Jesus is altogether wonderful: He is the Savior of the sinful, the Burden-Carrier for all who labor and are heavy laden, the Giver of Rest to the anxious, the Sin-Eater, the Prince of Peace who gives the troubled His perfect peace, and the Storm-Calmer who walks out on water to lift the sinking. Jesus is the head of God's family who never leaves, the one always seeking to bless and strengthen His people.

Jesus is the example we need to grow in our own God-given calling.

The Call to Courage: Act Like Men

One of the most humorous attacks I have observed on manhood goes something like this: "It is wrong to tell men to be tough and man up!" Such a critique frequently comes alongside a call for men to confess their "toxicity," as we have referenced throughout this book. Perhaps this sounds right. Here is what we should know from Scripture, though: men very much do need to show courage and toughness. We saw this in King David's dying charge to his son Solomon, when he told him, "Be strong, and show yourself a man" (1 Kings 2:2). We find a remarkably similar charge in 1 Corinthians 16:13–14.

Writing to a struggling church in ancient Corinth, Paul reinforces David's kingly summons. Paul urges the Corinthians to "Be watchful, stand firm in the faith, act like men, be strong. Let all that you do be done in love." This particular section is not given only to men, so it applies to all believers. But it also informs our understanding of strong manhood. Men, after all, were called by God to be the elders, shepherds, and apostles of the New Testament Church (more on that below). Men, therefore, had the responsibility of exercising the kind of character delineated here. This is especially true because Paul gave the command to "act like men" in the face of challenges to the Body of Christ.

Paul actually coined a Greek word here: *andrizesthe*. The concept of being manly, of demonstrating masculinity, motivated a Spirit-powered apostle to create this term. "Act like men" means numerous realities: not being a boy, not being a woman. But it especially means that a man must demonstrate courage. What a needed word for our day, when boys are encouraged—whether implicitly or explicitly—to lean back. This is not what the Scripture says to boys, young men, and men. In the power of the Spirit, Paul is essentially telling the Corinthians to "Man up!" His call is not to accept defeat or embrace passivity, but to reject such postures and live in the strength of God.

Paul is calling the Church to courage. Further, he is calling men to lead out in showing it. The five elements of his charge in verses 13–14 make sense when taken together and help us understand both godly faith and strong manhood. We must not be irresponsible, but "watchful," remembering that threats to God's people—to us individually—exist everywhere. As we have seen, we do not live in peacetime, but in spiritual war. Like the night watchman patrolling the wall of the city, we must constantly scan the horizon of our hearts and our minds, remaining vigilant (see Proverbs 4:23). We must not waver in our Christian commitment but "stand firm." We are called to be "immovable," not easily knocked off course, not crumbling to powder when opposed by the lightest touch. We must, furthermore, "be strong." Finally, this way of life is not driven by hate, but is motivated by love.

Paul did not think of himself as strong and courageous in his own power. Throughout his writings, in fact, he described himself as "weak" (2 Corinthians 11:29). Here we get at the paradox of strong biblical manhood. We are called to be strong—but even as we seek to practice strong manhood, we remember at all times that we can only pursue and practice it by the work of God in us. We are not Stoics, like the ancient Greeks who embraced their own code of self-denial for the honor of self. Nor are we self-made men.

In truth, we ourselves are very weak, but we serve a God who is very strong. This God does not bottle up His strength and keep it from us, but in His kindness lavishes it on His Church. The biblical God makes us "more than conquerors" by giving us all the indwelling

Spirit (Romans 8:37). By living a life of prayerful dependence and humble trust, God uses us in ways we would never think possible. So on the one hand, we are called to be strong, and by God's grace, we *are*. But on the other hand, we never lose sight of the fact that we are weak, and that God's power is made perfect in our weakness (see 2 Corinthians 12:8).

As we are at pains to say: take away God, and our strength collapses. We are all like Samson in this regard. There simply is no true lasting strength outside of God. Should we pursue courage and spiritual power as men? Yes, we must. But unlike what our culture tells us from numerous directions, we cannot look inside ourselves for our empowerment. We must look to God. Then and only then can we honor the Lord; then and only then can we *act like men*.

Men In Leadership:
The (Forgotten) Order of Creation

As we have seen, in the home, God has called men to be the heads of their wives. This means that men have authority from God to lead their home, and that wives are called to submit to this leadership. The call to leadership extends beyond the home, however. In the church, God has called men to be elders, pastors, and shepherds (these roles are one, in truth), and this means that God calls women to submit to male leadership in the church as well. This is not arbitrary. In 1 Timothy 2, Paul bases this ecclesial principle on the order of creation itself:

I do not permit a woman to teach or to exercise authority over a man; rather, she is to remain quiet. For Adam was formed first, then Eve; and Adam was not deceived, but

the woman was deceived and became a transgressor.
(1 Timothy 2:12–14)

The man was formed first by God, Paul teaches here, and as such was put in the position of spiritual authority. This is what we call "creation order." In the beginning, the man was not deceived as Eve was, Paul adds, which signals that Eve should not have been in the position she was. Men are not beyond being deceived, but they are called to stand between their wives and lies. They have been formed by God for this role, and are not called the "weaker vessel" as women are (1 Peter 3:6). Men are made, as we have observed repeatedly, to exercise strength on behalf of others. This is what elders of the church must do. They have the God-given responsibility of preaching, teaching, shepherding, and protecting the flock of Jesus Christ.

We cannot miss the significance of this teaching on the order of creation.[3] The Word of God calls men in some form to leadership in public life; we think of how Isaiah 3:12 comments on the sad plight of Israel.

My people—infants are their oppressors,
and women rule over them.
O my people, your guides mislead you
and they have swallowed up the course of your paths.

This text does not mean that a woman cannot lead in a business, school, or political endeavors. It does mean, however, that in a healthy society, men will step forward and lead. They will not lean back, asking women to do the hard work and heavy lifting. Instead, they will take on the burden of leadership. They will sacrifice to help and bless others. They will stand against evil and promote what is good. All this owes to the order of creation—to the man being formed first.

At this point, some men may be nodding. This material may be resonating. But perhaps some of you came of age when holding a feminist (or egalitarian) mindset, and now you wonder how you are supposed to live out the biblical model, not the cultural one. I'll say more in the closing application, but for now, here are a few priorities:

- Teach your family biblical truth through family devotions on a regular basis
- Join a church that stands upon the Word of God and teaches biblical manhood and womanhood
- Talk with your wife about how Scripture has transformed your worldview
- Listen to where she is, and pray with her
- Ask the Lord to lead your family to unity in truth
- Calmly and patiently lead in making changes in your roles and family life
- Where things get sticky and disagreements persist, go slow, use patience, and consider talking with a biblical counselor to seek oneness

The nice thing about writing a book is that you can be idealistic. You can tie things up neatly with a bow. But that's not real life. Real life is messy. If the Lord is opening your eyes to true biblical manhood (and true biblical womanhood), you will need to trust God to bring reformation and healing and change to your family.

This may take time, and there may be some real challenges along the way. But don't lose heart: God will honor those who honor His Word (1 Samuel 12:30). God will help you. God will lead you. As you draw your family into sound doctrine through patient instruction and wise leadership, you can trust God to work. His Word will not return void (Isaiah 55:11). But you will need to move at a pace that your loved ones can follow. If your wife has held more of a cultural mindset, you don't want to slash and burn. You want to pray much, lead calmly, admit past wrongs, and graciously forge a new direction for your family. Humility will help greatly here.

A man leading his family is no small matter. Satan has staked a great deal, in fact, on undermining male headship. He hates God's creation order. He hates when men reject secular thinking and embrace God's good design by the working of divine grace. But God loves this reorientation. God loves it when we honor His good purposes in creating the human race as He did. God made the man first and invested him with great agency and responsibility. He did not rob women of dignity in doing so; to the contrary, as we have seen, a woman being her husband's "helper" means that she brings valuable skills, abilities, and words to the relationship.

The woman's role is essential, but the man has the call from God to lead. It is written into his constitution. It is formed in his nature. He cannot make it otherwise, nor can any gender theorist, politician, human resources administrator, celebrity, or activist. When we live out this design by the grace of God, we flourish. When we reject it and try to revise it, we struggle.

Men As Watchmen on the Wall: The Multifaceted Godliness of the Elder

As is clear, men have been given a high and holy responsibility from God. Serving as an overseer or elder, Paul writes to his disciple Timothy that an elder should be a man who is above reproach, the husband of one wife, sober-minded, self-controlled, respectable, hospitable, able to teach, not a drunkard, not violent but gentle, not quarrelsome, not a lover of money. (1 Timothy 3:2–3)

The man who would lead the church is first and foremost a godly man. His life is disciplined and controlled by the Spirit. He is not a wild man; he is not untamed or careening. He is solid and steady. His whole walk with Christ is aboveboard; you cannot easily accuse him of rebellion, for he is "above reproach." He thinks carefully ("sober-minded") and is not rash or hasty. He does not act immaturely or basely but is "respectable." He opens his home to others ("hospitable") and is generous. He can teach the Word to others, and his life backs up what he teaches.[4]

In truth, what we call self-rule characterizes this leader. Here we see the nature of strong men: they are not those who do whatever they want whenever they want and beat their chests about it. Strong men are those who have come under the control of God's rule. Their whole life is a life of strength, but not necessarily through brute feats and death-defying stunts. The strength of the godly man has many dimensions but is at base applied by the grace of God to his sin and character. Instead of being a "drunkard," divine grace keeps him under discipline. Instead of being "violent" with a hair-trigger temper, divine grace enables him to be "gentle." Instead of picking fights for no good reason, the work of divine grace means he is "not quarrelsome" but peaceable. Instead of spending money like water or ordering his life to acquire riches, divine grace frees him from the love of money.

The same godly strength impacts the lives of his loved ones. He manages the home well, and his children learn discipline from his example (vv. 4–5). He cannot be a recent convert, or else he will fall prey to the wildness of conceit (v. 6). The elder is not known for immorality or evil behavior, and he steers well clear of anything that might "disgrace" himself or, far more importantly, his God (v. 7).

The devil, Paul indicates, has laid a "snare" for this man and every man. He wants strong men to act like angry men. This is no impossible achievement; it tragically happens regularly. All of us carry the seeds of our own destruction within us. The elder must always mind this truth, step carefully, and live wisely. He will not act perfectly, and we cannot expect that of him. But he does, in general terms, live in the strength of God's power applied to all the unruly areas of his mind, heart, and soul.

The character of the elder as laid out by Paul gives men a benchmark. Whether or not our church asks us to serve in this role is not the point; it is that the New Testament gives us guidance, color, and perspective on godly male character. The citation above gives an essential word about self-control. Self-control is not the absence of strength; it is strength under control by the power of God.

This is why, in this book, I have used the term "self-rule" in numerous places. The man who is strongest is not the one who bullies others, brutalizes those around him when they offend him, and generally keeps people in a state of fear. Such a man is weak—very weak. By the grace of God, it is the self-ruled man—embodied by the church's male elders—who show the world what true strength is.

True strength comes from God, and true strength means that a man is not ruled by his appetites, desires, and passions, but rather rules them. If this sounds like the opposite of passivity and sinful weakness, it's because it is. Steve Lawson has concisely captured the nature of this biblical concept: "Self-rule brings every thought, word, and deed captive to the obedience of Christ (2 Cor. 10:5). Any advance in personal holiness demands self-control."[5]

The crucible in which this character is formed is first the family and then the congregation. Of course, we know from other biblical passages that godly men are not always married. As 1 Corinthians 7 shows, there is a clear place for singleness in the church. God calls some men to singleness, and for good reason:

> The unmarried man is anxious about the things of the Lord, how to please the Lord. But the married man is anxious about worldly things, how to please his wife, and his interests are divided. (1 Corinthians 7:32–34)

Paul does not teach that marriage is bad in this section; his normative expectation of elders, after all, is that they will be married and have children. But singleness that is given to God and thus lived for God's glory is a blessing to Him and His people. The single man can devote himself to the things of the Lord uninterruptedly. This is a great testimony in a world where too many men choose singleness for the complete opposite reason: they want to live life without any bonds, duties, or attachments.

For that reason, we need to distinguish between worldly singleness and godly singleness. A worldly life is devoted to self, in some form; a godly life is given over to the Lord. Men do not need to marry to be strong men of God. Thus, the church needs to teach a robust concept of singleness.

But we must also make clear that most men are called to marriage, and that as such, marriage and child-raising form a key part of a man's maturation process before God. Further, we want young men to step forward and pursue marriage as they perceive (with help) that God would have them marry. In an age of delayed maturity, our churches must not assume that godly men will know to move in this direction of their own volition. Our culture has in many cases jackhammered up the script of marriage and family. Young men need help finding it—wisdom in knowing how to engage young women well, and shepherding in their journey as husbands and fathers.

Many men are struggling today, but there is great hope before us. The world is breaking men down, but God is building them back up. He is still in the business of making weak men strong. God is empowering single men to show the world that our hearts are only truly satisfied in Him. He is enabling young men—including many from divorced homes or troubled backgrounds—to take on the vocational roles of leader, protector, and provider. The godly man must lead and manage his home well. He must nourish his wife in a Christlike way. And as Paul teaches in 1 Timothy 5:8, he must "provide for his relatives, and especially for members of his household," for if he does not, "he has denied the faith and is worse than an unbeliever."

God wants men to work, and work hard. He wants us to train our sons to shoulder the burden of providing for the family. We think here of how, in the same epistle to Timothy we have covered above, Paul urges young widows not to take up a vocation to earn money, but to "marry, bear children, manage their households, and give the adversary no occasion for slander" (1 Timothy 5:14). The world has made it possible for men to withdraw from providing. But God wants them to work hard. Working for provision is a big part of becoming and showing oneself a man. Provision makes every family member's God-given order possible and enjoyable. As with so many matters, we need to restore the goodness and dignity of masculine provision.

Conclusion

We have covered a great deal of material in this chapter and may well come away from this study feeling our inadequacy. In truth, it is—as we have stated several times—only by the grace of God that any man can live out His perfectly wise plan for men. Biblical manhood is not something we embody in our own strength; like all the Christian life, it depends upon the transforming and sanctifying grace of God for its existence and endurance.

Praise God, we Christian men need not feel condemned when we fail. We should repent, and we should confess our sin. Then we should get back to business, striving to grow in areas where we are weak. At no point, however, should we embrace "our feminine side" or become an effeminate man. Not for us the model of Mr. Mom; that is a modern invention from the pagan mind, ultimately, not the ancient call issued from the sacred book. We are not women; we have no "feminine side"; we are all called to be men with many dimensions, many traits, many developing abilities. This, and not *soft manhood*, is what God expects of us.

God has made us men, and it is good and right that He has done so. But He does not only want us to acknowledge the plain and obvious fact of our masculinity; He wants us to get our hands dirty in the world he has made. He wants us to live as men, to enjoy being men of God, and to take dominion of what He has entrusted to us. Much of what I have laid out goes against the urgings of many influential voices in our culture. But living out God's design brings great glory and honor to our Creator and Redeemer.

By His grace, let us choose the better way—whatever it may cost us.

CHAPTER 7

The Physical Distinctiveness of Men

But I discipline my body and keep it under control,
lest after preaching to others I myself should be
disqualified.

Apostle Paul

It is a true, if strange, story: A boy was being raised by two lesbians in a post-gender home. All the supposed toxicities of traditional American masculinity were being flushed out of this little guy; no traces of patriarchy would remain. He would be a rainbow boy in a rainbow family. To carry out this plan, the boy had no access to guns, superheroes, or violence of any kind. He was not only post-gender; he was post-stereotype of any kind. The entire project revolved around the very modern idea that we choose our own identities and bear no imprint within us that directs our behavior. We choose our own sexuality and gender identity. But not just this: we choose that of our children, too.

There was just one problem: the boy had some very boy-like tendencies. Though he had no toy guns and watched no shoot-'em-up cartoons, he still shocked his lesbian "mothers" one day when he was eating breakfast. He took his toast and very carefully bit off strategic pieces of it. Then, after he had shaped it into the form he wanted, he sat back, admiring his masterpiece: a gun. Specifically, a toast-gun. That's right: this boy, deprived of masculine influences, cut off from play combat, still had war and danger hardwired into him. An unassuming piece of bread morphed into a gun. Welcome to the wonder of boys.

On a more serious note, I have no doubt that there are many children today whose parents are tragically carrying out the same foul effort. I grieve for that, and I am sure many others do as well. But this anecdote nonetheless gives me hope. It reminds me that God's design is strong. The architecture of manhood is not weak. God has written it into boys' bones and bloodstreams to be boyish. Such wiring is not bad or even neutral. It is good for boys to be boys, and for men to be men. In fact, the very makeup of a boy will usher him in the direction of manhood.

There is a one-word reason for much of this instinctual progression: testosterone.

The Bodies of Men: A Cornucopia of Distinctiveness

In the age of science, it is truly shocking how much we are asked to believe about men that is anything but scientific. We hear that men should be more like women; that women and men are basically the same in their makeup; that boys should not be encouraged to be men in the traditional physical sense; that girls should play sports with boys; that men who have a cross-gender identity should be able to go into the women's bathroom; that a man can "transition" his body into a female body; that society should not promote masculine standards of fitness for the military but lower them to make them more accessible. All this supposed rational "science" carries not an ounce of truth in it.

In the physical sense, we need to start with the very basics. Though each are fully human, men and women are different in the most basic physical way: at the level of DNA. The father determines the sex of a child, with baby boys getting a Y chromosome for an XY genotype, and baby girls getting an X chromosome for an XX genotype. Mothers only give their children X chromosomes. At the risk of overstating the obvious, having a Y chromosome means the child will develop a penis. Without it, the child will develop a vagina and breasts that can potentially nurse a baby.

The preceding paragraph would not have caused controversy in most any society since the dawn of time. But in our day, it will likely draw the label of "cisgender hate speech" or some such thing. Yet we cannot help but repeat it: it is not hateful to state the simplest of biological realities about the human person. The opposite is true: it is deeply unloving to obscure these God-formed facts.

The truth is this: God made both manhood and womanhood. As such, our manliness or womanliness is where the wonder rests. For our purposes, boys need to hear that their bodies are fearfully and wonderfully made by God, and as such, are not lying to them. If they have a boy's organs and a boy's frame, they are boys. There are not boys who have "girl parts"; boys are boys whether they feel like it on a given day or not. There is an absolute synchronicity between your identity and your body.

Before we move on, let me answer a possible objection at this point. What about babies born with both male and female genitalia? Don't they show that the "binary gender" worldview is wrong? In a word, no. The child born with such a condition—sometimes called "intersex," best called a Disorder of Sex Development (DSD)—has sadly suffered a bodily effect of Adam's fall.[1] Sin has warped their precious body, in other words. But that child is still a boy or a girl, and this will be found in normal terms at the chromosomal level. If they have a XX genotype, then they should be raised as a girl, for they are one; if a XY genotype, they are a boy, and should be raised as one.

Thankfully, surgeons have the ability to help here, and the child need not suffer terrible and unresolved confusion as their life develops.[2]

So, to restate the point: even if the external frame is tragically warped, the body still speaks. God has written our identity as a man or a woman into our DNA. These statements are important because we live in an age when feelings, to a large extent, are allowed to determine one's reality. Christians need to have a strong voice in responding to such a view. We know why we have feelings; we have them because God gave them to us. The true purpose of our feelings is that we would experience in the deepest and most holistic way the love of God. Though feelings are a gift from God, they must be ruled by Him. If they are not, they have the potential to upend our existence, confuse us, and lead us away from the biblical model of the self. A culture that tries to ground its identity in its feelings, as ours does, sets us all up for great disaster—and for eternal peril besides.

We must be clear on this: feelings are not the ground of our identity. God has written and fixed that for us through our biology. We are not autonomous selves. We are dependent creatures. We are also distinct creatures from one another.

Let us consider several of the meaningful physical differences between men and women.[3]

Seven More Differences between Men and Women

Sight

Men have better depth perception, distance vision, and see more clearly in lighted environments. But when it comes to night vision, visual memory, and the red end of the spectrum, women excel. Men are ten times more likely to be colorblind than women; women blink twice as often as men. Perhaps this is why, when we see a strong leader who rarely blinks, his self-possession stands out.

Size

In general, men are about 10 percent bigger than women.[4] This begins in infancy and carries throughout life. Their larger size speaks of men's natural duty to protect women and children. To put this in elemental terms, if a big threat comes, the biggest (and strongest) person should respond. That is usually the man.

Strength. It's hard to find an exact number to mark the gap here. But estimates show that on average, men have around 30–40 percent more upper body strength than women.[5] That is a remarkable reality. It stems from the man's frame; his shoulders are wider, his chest is thicker, and his upper body in general is constituted not for nurturing children by way of the breasts, but for work and bearing burdens.

The modern entertainment complex rejects this fact. In more contemporary movies and shows than you can count, the female protagonist—usually petite and thin, perhaps weighing 120 pounds— savages the male warriors and fighters who battle her. Of course, some women have serious strength and ferocity, but on average, men are much stronger than women. This is why we have separate teams for boys and girls, men and women. We want to protect the fairer sex from danger and harm. The society that collapses such distinctions is anything but "pro-woman"; the one that honors God-given distinctions between the sexes is the one that actually acts on women's behalf.

Quality of Health and Length of Life

Anyone who has been told that men have the game rigged in their favor on all counts needs to study some science (the genuine article). On average, women live five years longer than men. According to some sources, women's adrenal glands enable them to resist disease more effectively than men due to the extra cortin they produce. In general, aside from a few serious illnesses, men die more often than women from the major diseases like cancer and heart troubles.[6]

You can track the differing life expectancy of the sexes through funny videos with titles like "Why Men Die Young." Certainly, men do not always help themselves with their life choices (see below on testosterone). However, we must also point out that many men take on a great deal in order to help and bless others. In general terms, men go to war; men protect communities; men do hard and dirty jobs no one else wants to do—jobs that keep society running and communities functioning. These and other commitments put men in greater danger. Some people respond by urging us to retrain boys' masculine instincts. But it is here that we are reminded: some significant part of men's fulfillment comes from risk, from challenges, from hardship. In order for a man to thrive, he needs not the absence of difficulty, but its presence. He needs odds to overcome.

Organs and Bones

Men have larger hearts and lungs than women. Women, by contrast, have bigger stomachs, livers, and kidneys than men. Their hearts beat faster than those of men. Women have wider hips, a longer trunk, and shorter legs than men.[7] While we would not want to over-read these physical differences, we should not underplay them, either. Men's greater heart and lung capacity speaks to the calling we have sketched throughout this book: Men have been given greater physical capacity for tasks related (at least historically) to provision and protection. Women's bodies on average are not as adapted to such work. Their wider hips instead speak to the ability to bear children, though of course not every woman will.

Spatial Skills

Studies show men tend to be better at navigating through space and using mechanical reasoning.[8] For example, one study showed four out of five men are better at assessing velocity than women. Similarly,

> Boys and men have corresponding advantages in throwing distance, velocity, and accuracy. Jardine and Martin (1983) provided an early demonstration of this sex difference when they found that about seven out of eight adolescent boys threw more accurately at a non-moving object than did the average same-age girl, whereas nine out of ten of their fathers threw more accurately than their mothers.[9]

This study—and others like it—backs up an anecdotal assessment of men's strengths. Worldwide, sports show that men generally excel at movement in space. The prevalence of men in fields involving mechanical reasoning backs up the same contention. This does not, as some allege, reflect nurturing or environmental conditioning alone, but something much deeper: the very design of God. This design does not make men better than women, but it does make them different and gifted in certain ways for certain tasks, just as the reverse holds.

Compartmentalization

If you conduct an internet search on this topic, you will find several resources saying how negative it is that men tend to cordon their emotions off from the rest of their lives. There's a degree of truth here: The masculine instinct to compartmentalize (focusing narrowly on a given task or topic) can certainly prove harmful. Men can and do suppress their emotions in sinful and harmful ways, and so from a young age, boys need to be trained to process, understand, and handle their emotions.

But compartmentalization is actually vital. It is a key part of what allows men to focus on work duties, undertake great missions, and face terrible odds without wilting. You could call it by a different name: single-mindedness. We think, for example, of men who go to war to conquer evil and keep their loved ones safe. Those men must stifle certain emotions and needs for a long time in order to stay focused on the task at hand. As at war, so in daily life. Compartmentalization can yield negative results, yes, but it can also be a definite strength, albeit one men must always seek to steward well.

Sexual Capacity and Interest

Men on average have stronger sex drives than women. People vary, of course, and we should not read women having lower libido in general as a sign that they do not have any meaningful sexual interest. Nor in terms of the ministry of the church should we treat sexual passions as an issue only for men. Nonetheless, men's sex drive is higher than women's in broad perspective. The peak of a woman's sex drive is influenced by her menstrual cycle, while men's are not so seasonal. While women see significant decreases in their fertility after age thirty-five, men can father children into their seventies. At the physical level, females have more erogenous zones than males.

So too is sex itself different for many men and women: for men, the act is in general a matter of surging desire and physical release, while for women, the act is more multidimensional, proceeding from a general sense of closeness and intimacy across categories. These differences help us unpack the biblical plan for sex. It is not a fast-food good that anyone can have at any time. Sex is a complex and even complicated gift from God. It is made for joy, pleasure, and marital unity of the most intimate kind. But as in other areas of marriage, the way this occurs is not by pretending no differing desires or opinions exist. It is by husband and wife communicating with one another, better understanding one another, and working hard to love one another well in this regard. Don't believe Hollywood regarding sex: like all of marriage, it takes work, patience, practice, and love.

The Power and Utility of Testosterone

When I speak on manhood at a church or a conference, I usually stop before we get deep into the material to ask a simple question: Who has heard about the role of testosterone in the lives of boys and men? Usually a few hands go up, but very few. Then I ask a follow-up: Who knows, on average, how much more testosterone men have on average than women? I usually get blank faces. When I give the number, people often gasp aloud: According to estimates from the Mayo Clinic, men generally have around 2,000 percent more testosterone than women.[10] Harvard lecturer Carole Hooven generally concurs: "Both sexes produce [testosterone], but men have ten to twenty times as much as women."[11]

This data matters tremendously. It shows us, off the bat, just how distinct manhood is. Both men and women have estrogen and testosterone, of course. But testosterone is pivotal in the physical formation and makeup of men—it is primarily produced in the male sex organs, the testicles. Like serotonin and oxytocin, it does not only show up in one sex, and it affects both sexes throughout their lives. But when puberty begins per the intricate design of our Creator God, boys' testosterone levels skyrocket. This is why, to the chagrin of every single teenage boy who has ever lived, his voice cracks and then deepens. It is why he develops facial hair, body hair, acne for several blissful years, and muscle where previously there was none.

Surging testosterone is also why his burgeoning interest in girls grows as well. (So blame testosterone for the pop music industry, basically.) His body and his mind work together on this count to develop what we call a "sex drive." He has sexual interest in the opposite sex, and experiences erections and the production of sperm and seminal fluid. None of this stems from the young man willing this into being; God is the one who has written this code and detailed this script. He has done so, we hasten to add, in a complementary way in young women. No scientist or gender theorist came up with these processes; no evolutionary biologist mapped out this marvelous metamorphosis. All this comes from God, owes to God, and—stewarded rightly—glorifies God.

Several of the changes noted above proceed from this pubertal explosion. At younger ages, boys and girls compete at relatively the same level. But when puberty strikes, boys' ability and aggression shoots through the roof because their testosterone levels are now twenty times higher than those in girls. Here is what this creates, as one authority has testified:

> The striking male postpubertal increase in circulating testosterone provides a major, ongoing, cumulative, and durable physical advantage in sporting contests by creating larger and stronger bones, greater muscle mass and strength, and higher circulating hemoglobin as well as possible psychological (behavioral) differences. In concert, these render women, on average, unable to compete effectively against men in power-based or endurance-based sports.[12]

Simply put, men have a physical advantage over women in contact sports. On average, men run faster, jump higher, and can accomplish harder athletic tasks.[13] This is not because of education or access to resources, but divine creational intent. Men have been made by God as the stronger, not the weaker, sex. Men excel in competitive environments because God made them to excel in them.

At the level of science and biology, we see God's intent in the disproportionate testosterone levels of men and women. The sexes were not made to be the same, they are not presently the same, and they never will be the same. Testosterone is a major part of this distinctiveness. It shapes boys sexually and in numerous other ways.

Testosterone accounts for at least two other sizeable dimensions of a man's existence: aggression and risk-taking, each of which we now examine. Michael Gurian is an expert on boys. He is not a born-again Christian, but he has studied boys in depth and gives a good sense for how testosterone drives their aggression:

> A little boy (on average) will turn toys into guns or swords with more frequency than girls will. He will hit more. He will try to one-up more. He will tend less toward empathic first responses to others' pain and more toward provocative first responses. He will be generally more competitive than his sister and especially in the few activities in which he perceives the potential to dominate over or be superior in. He will assess his potential to dominate based on his understanding of his personality, talent, and skill strengths. He will seek rough-and-tumble play or, if he perceives himself as physically weak, another outlet for aggression.[14]

Gurian does not argue that all of these instinctual behaviors should receive commendation. Nor would I. But before we jump to our efforts to mold boys morally and spiritually, we need to consider his wise summation. According to him, boys are *dominated* by testosterone. It is not a small and glancing feature of their makeup. If one wishes to crack the masculine code, understanding the dominance of testosterone helps greatly. Testosterone makes boys aggressive. It makes them hit other people for no good reason, as any father or mother can attest. It causes them to try to outdo one another or other children. It drives them away from empathy and toward insensitivity. It magnifies a boy's superiority in given areas, making him want to exploit that ability still more. It causes him to perceive the world as a contest, and for him to calculate where he can most succeed.

As we can see already (and will continue to explore), it is hard to overstate the importance of testosterone in the lives of boys and men. We could put it this way: If you do not grasp this reality, you will not understand men. Further, you will think that you can socially reengineer them when you cannot—and must not—do so. There is a better way forward: Instead of trying to rewire boys and change their boyish nature, we should study them, shepherd them, and help them.

Testosterone and Risk-Taking

We can help boys greatly by comprehending how testosterone relates to risk-taking. Contra our anti-male culture, this is a key part of masculine thinking and behavior. Failing to recognize and even celebrate this means we will raise malformed men, a sad outcome that—as we saw earlier—is a goal many nonetheless actively pursue today.

Gurian speaks well to the role of the effect of testosterone in this area of a man's life:

When he becomes an adult, you can expect him to be more aggressive and competitive than the average woman—remember, we are again speaking of averages—more ambitious about workplace superiority; more prone to one-up in

conversation; quicker to react physically to external stimu-
lation. He will be more likely to hit when he feels accosted,
and to seek rough-and-tumble play, competitive sports,
or any physical or motor activities through which he can
release tension, take risks, and show competitive prowess.[15]

If we can simplify this helpful summary, we could say this: testosterone makes men try hard things. Instead of embracing a placid
experience, testosterone drives them toward suffering, hardship, and
difficulty.

Reading this from a theological angle means that God has made
men to take risks.

They do so neither by accident nor as a bygone archetype of
the Western imperialist past. Rather than being trained out of a
risk-taking mindset, we should train boys to risk well. We should
steward and shape their natural urges. We should help them handle
their instincts well, and always point them to the grace of God as
their ultimate strength.

The effect of testosterone in this dimension of existence is incon-
trovertible. Gurian points out:

> Testosterone so influences aggression and even assertive-
> ness that studies done on women have shown an increase
> in both qualities when women have been injected with
> testosterone-like androgenic hormones.... They take more
> risks, discover more ambition within themselves and in the
> workplace, and feel more assertive in everyday life.[16]

In making these observations, we do not give a blank check to
men for their risk-taking nature. Yet it is also true that we must never
obliterate or erase God's design of them.

Risk-taking can produce all sorts of foolishness. I remember going to the local pizza shop when I was a teen, uncapping the pepper, and blowing into it through my soda straw as hard as I could. I did it only because a pretty girl sat opposite me, and my testosterone-washed brain thought drawing attention—even for something stupid—would improve my standing with her better than sitting quietly and waiting for my pepperoni pizza to arrive. Being an undisciplined young man, I took a risk, but it was a very bad one, and it led to a painful trip to the local eye doctor, who had the joy of removing numerous pieces of pepper straight from my eyeball.

Risking can be silly, as this shows. But risk-taking may serve much better ends, too. We find testosterone put to good use when a young man fastens on a vocation he wishes to try. Testosterone is put to good use when he takes the risk of pursuing a young woman's heart. (In such moments, many of us need all the help we can get, including biochemical help.) Testosterone is put to good use when a man changes up his family's situation when his loved ones are flagging, perhaps because of a church that is drifting from sound doctrine. We need and must have men who are not only *willing* to take these and other kinds of risks, but are *ready* to do so.

In this area and so many others, young men need discipleship, not denunciation. They need love and investment, not rewiring and neglect. When a young man acts well, he needs affirmation of that action. When he acts poorly, he needs reasoned analysis and calm instruction. But as fathers and mothers, we should never want to stop our boys from being boyish. We should never want to cleanse them of testosterone so they never break anything. We should never want to medicate them so that they live in a pacified state. Making boys timid is not a victory. Ridding the earth of manliness is not a triumph.

As we are at pains to say, testosterone itself is not the problem; boys are not the problem; *sin* is the problem. We should not unman our boys, as our culture demands. Instead, we should do the harder and deeper work: We should pay attention to them. We should love them. We should point them to Christ. In deep affection and commitment, we should train them, help them, and never leave them.

How Adrenaline Keeps Us Safe

We actually need young men to be who they are. As we have seen, in a unique way, God made men to respond to danger. We see this happening all across Scripture, and we also see it when we study the workings of the male body and brain. In their seminal study *Why Men Don't Iron*, Bill and Anne Moir articulate the power of adrenaline:

> The human response to challenge is better known as the fear, flight, or fight mechanism, and it is triggered by an adrenalin rush. The adrenal gland produces adrenalin and noradrenalin, and these substances are crucial if we are to respond to the challenge at maximum efficiency. The adrenalin rush is a summons to battle stations; it sends energy to the muscles and shuts down biological functions that are not crucial to the moment, which is why men shot in battle frequently do not remember any pain at the moment of wounding. The adrenalin rush adapts us to deal with imminent danger, and without it we would be far more likely to fail the challenge. Men's adrenal response is much larger than women's.[17]

Alongside testosterone, adrenaline helps us understand men. It is not that women don't possess it, but men have a "much larger" capacity for it. Adrenaline does not filter down in unnoticeable drips;

it rushes upon men, rousing the entire body, sending it surging into the fray. This is not a conscious choice. No matter what the gender theorists tell us, men have been given this innate working from God. We are ready for action already as men, and adrenaline only readies us further.

This shows us a crucial truth: God does not want us to shy away from action and danger. He has created us to meet the real threats around us, equipped us to meet them head on, and—even if wounded—to keep pounding forward.

As noted, adrenaline enhances men's ability to compartmentalize. This propensity, which has driven wives batty for millennia, serves as both a weakness and a strength. We sometimes fail to engage our wives holistically, wrongly assuming that a quick conversation has addressed their concerns, and move on breezily to something else. That is no strength.

But our compartmentalization faculty also enables us to deal with problems in a direct manner. It lets us drop the baggage that might destabilize us and tackle challenges aggressively. Like testosterone, adrenaline shapes men. It makes us fierce and even ruthless—qualities that a fallen world makes necessary in certain ways. It causes men to focus intensely on issues before us. It keeps us from getting cloudy and helps us zero in on problems that must be solved with single-minded concentration for the good of our loved ones.

Men want to focus on something intensely because we have a natural draw to action. As one example, Bill and Anne Moir capture why many men like sports so much:

Men need sport in ways that women do not. PET (positive emission tomography) scanners have shown that even when a man is relaxing his brain, unlike hers, continues to show high activity in those parts which control movement and aggression. His mind is restless, always ready for action, and sports provide that; which is why, to relax, he can watch hours of sport. He becomes one with the flow of the action: advance, retire, hold, pass—attack, attack, attack. This is him: his hormones and brain are at one—at peace.[18]

Take heart, women who endure much sports-watching in the home: men who love athletic contests, among other pursuits and interests, are simply living out their neurochemistry. As with all facets of manhood, this instinct needs spiritual reorientation. Many of us men can surely watch far too much sports, this is true (I may have just cleared my throat). But ignoring the natural wiring of men, with our innate appetite for aggressive competition, is also a bad move. Our natural wiring as men should not be reprogrammed, so that we live against nature; our natural wiring should instead be spiritually transformed, so that we live according to nature by the grace of God.

Conclusion

Boys need help in many ways—but the help they need today is in many senses the opposite of the "help" our culture would provide them. Boys do not need to be treated like girls, nor should they be identified with girls, as if they have no distinctiveness. Boys should not be asked to be girls. Boys are made by God. They have a great deal of distinctiveness. Even if boys go through an unfortunate and cruel reeducation project, they will still live out their distinctiveness—even by the way they bite their toast.

Boys' bodily distinctiveness need not be a threat or a problem. When approached with great respect for God's design and great love for our boys, it can instead be a real source of joy, laughter, and growth. Boys are not the problem, at the end of the day. They do sin and need real shepherding and spiritual formation. But boys who receive much love and investment, and who know the grace of God to overcome their sin and failings, represent nothing less than the future of the family, the Church, the community, and the world beyond. In serious measure, as boys go, so goes the world.

This truth represents a real challenge for us, for boys can surely be a handful. But the discipling of God-designed boys is not a burden; it is a delightful undertakingand nothing less than a calling from God.

CHAPTER 8

The Social
Distinctiveness of Men

Masculinity must prove itself, and do so before an audience.

Harvey Mansfield Jr.

To this day, the most shocking intellectual confrontation I have ever witnessed was between Cathy Newman, a journalist with Channel 4 News in the UK, and Jordan Peterson. I had heard of Peterson, but he was a relatively unknown professor in Toronto, and like many, I hadn't closely tracked him. But this one interview changed all that. Before it, Peterson was obscure; after it, Peterson became the leading voice in the West against leftist ideology.

Newman tried, over and over, to paint Peterson as an evil patriarchist. A very bright woman with a cutting conversational style, she repeatedly made the argument—from different angles—that the working world is dominated by men and thus unfair to women. Peterson spoke more as a cultural observer than a prophet most of the time; he simply observed that men gravitate to the hardest and thus highest-paying jobs. As a feminist, Newman doggedly tried to translate Peterson's observations into an anti-woman stance, but he slipped the trap every single time. See this exchange, for example:

> Newman: Feminine traits. Why are they not desirable at the top?
>
> Peterson: It's hard to say. I'm just laying out the empirical evidence. We know the traits that predict success.
>
> Newman: But we also know because companies by and large have not been dominated by women over the centuries. We have nothing to compare it to. It's an experiment.
>
> Peterson: True. And it could be the case that if companies modified their behavior and became more feminine, they would be successful. But there's no evidence for it.
>
> Newman: You seem doubtful about that.
>
> Peterson: I'm not neither doubtful nor nondoubtful. There's no evidence for it.[1]

This strange crossfire reminds us as Christians that to stand for manhood in any form today puts you in the cultural penalty box. This is even more the case when we speak of it in theological terms, not just psychological ones. Small wonder that many Christians say little about this subject, for it has been super-heated as a matter of cultural controversy. Indeed, when Satan wants the truth to be quieted, he makes even discussing it "controversial."

As men of God, though, we cannot fall silent. We must define manhood both biblically and practically. We must show how it is distinctive from womanhood so the next generation would know how to understand and embody it. Having explored biblical manhood across several previous chapters, now we connect the dots and ask this: In a day-to-day sense, how does manhood flesh itself out in our activities and decisions?

15 Realities of Strong Manhood

Men Aren't Women

As Genesis 1 and Matthew 19:4 make clear, men are not women. Yet it is amazing how so many voices in our culture minimize the differences between the sexes—even in Christian circles. If you only read Twitter and blogs, you might think that manhood and womanhood are basically incidental matters—a matter of biology, nothing more.

But anyone who gets married, has children, or finds themselves in a family will know that these differences are not at all incidental in many respects. To understand ourselves and our world, we must boldly and unashamedly declare that men are not women. We need to be understood, honored, and appreciated as men. We do not want men to become women. We know that men in fact *cannot* become women, and even if they could, this would not fit God's design or glorify our Maker. Instead, we want boys to become men, and we want men to become strong in God.

But all this depends on a simple yet radical confession: men are not women. Men will thrive only when they unlock who they are as men and identify how they are to live as men. Such knowledge, as we have established, comes from the Word of God.

Men Aren't Boys

Just as men are not women, so they are not boys. Tucked in a discussion on prophecy and spiritual gifts, the Apostle Paul gives this clarifying word:

> When I was a child, I spoke like a child, I thought like a child, I reasoned like a child. When I became a man, I gave up childish ways. (1 Corinthians 13:11)

This verse cracks like thunder in the age of perpetual adolescence. It convicts us all. Men and boys both need it in a major way today. It makes sense for a child to be childlike; it makes no sense for an adult to be childlike.

Our challenge is to help our boys see that it is good to grow up. It is good to be a man. It is a joy to mature. It is healthy and right to leave behind childish speech, thinking, and reasoning. In a culture that lionizes being young forever, we want to communicate that God's glory lies in personal transformation. Does this mean you cannot enjoy sports and relaxation and recreation of various kinds? Not at all. But it does mean that boys need to see men who do not live their lives yearning for a time machine to go back to the glory days when they had no responsibilities, but instead press forward in faith and hope in God. Boyhood is not the goal; strong manhood is.

Men Love Jesus

Jesus must not be just a small part of our lives as men. If we are to be strong, we must know Him as our Lord and Savior. We may think we are strong naturally, and God may have given us certain innate abilities and capacities—but no man is strong enough to save himself. No man can make himself right before a holy God. No man can cleanse his sin or pay his debt to God. No man can be good enough, assertive enough, or life-hacked enough to give himself a new nature. For our spiritual condition, and for everything we face, we need Jesus.[2]

We must not view such a confession as a cop-out. Knowing Christ as our Savior does not end our journey as men. To the contrary, we have so very much to learn about manhood once we come to faith in Christ, and much of it centers on Christ Himself. On this count, we cannot miss that true manhood does not mean looking within; it means looking at Jesus, studying Him, learning from Him, and soaking up the wisdom of the Word of which He is the Alpha and the Omega. We must not form men who think they themselves are the answer to what ails us. They are no such thing. We need men who know they are sinful, know they are weak, and who look to God to make them strong by the power of the blood of His Son.

Men Confess Sin

True manhood does not mean never saying you're sorry or acting as if you are untouchable. It does not translate to aloofness. It certainly does not mean that you have everything figured out and need no help. True manhood for sinners like us means admitting you are sinful at your core. As David shows us in Psalm 51, it means confessing your sin to God, trusting in Christ, and then battling your sin all the rest of your days on Earth.

This is one of the biggest struggles for many of us men. We fight a lifelong conflict with our pride. Sin comes from our mind, our heart, our mouth, and our actions. We are depraved by nature, and we need to become totally new people. When we do trust Christ, we do not *stop* confessing and repenting of our sin; we have only begun a lifetime of such spiritual work. We have landed on one of the truly essential practices of our existence: that we be honest about our failings, confess them to God in repentant sorrow, and trust God to forgive us yet again.

The strongest men are not those who never admit any wrong. The strongest men are the ones who hide nothing from God or man and tell the truth about their sins. Godly men must show strength in many ways. We rarely show more spiritual power than when, by the grace of God, we pray prayers of confession, tell our loved ones we were wrong, ask for forgiveness in those situations, and make clear to those around us that we are not the righteous rescuer appointed by God. Christ is.

Men Are Warriors

At root, men yearn to take on a great cause and be part of a worthy mission. This is because men have warrior wiring; God made Adam to lead in taking dominion and guarding the Garden of Eden from foes (Genesis 2:15). Due to this truth, our boys need to be raised as boys. They need an upbringing that fits their testosterone-driven physiology. They need a rearing that connects with their God-given wiring, with all the adventure and big-picture vision that God has placed in them. Boys are not made for passivity and listlessness. They are made for action. Wherever they go as they mature, they need to be trained like warriors are trained: with discipline, goals, and purpose.

Men who come to faith in Christ also need such shaping. You need not fight in combat to be a warrior, but you do need to approach your daily existence as though you are a warrior, for you are one. Whether you sit in front of a computer all day or cut timber with a saw almost as big as you are, prioritize discipline, goals, and purpose each day.

You can apply this in lots of areas: Don't just go to the gym, but have a target for yourself. Don't just punch the clock at work; labor *coram deo*, unto God and before God, as you strive to be excellent in your vocation. Don't just have children; be the best father you can by applying discipline to your schedule. Get home in time to see the kids. Save some energy for them. Beyond all this, approach your life as if you are a warrior, and watch as it sharpens and clarifies your daily pursuits.

Men Take Risks

What did God call Abraham to do in Genesis 12? "Go!" God said to him, and so Christ also said to His disciples in giving them the Great Commission (Matthew 28:16–20). Men must be *goers*, and that means they must take risks. Advancement entails risk in a fallen world. Yet many men today have lost their capacity for risk, for action, for bold faith. In a good number of cases, they have had such God-given instincts muted, rebuked, and drummed out of them. They fear leaving the nest, stepping out in faith, being humiliated.

In a safety-obsessed context, we must help boys and men recover a spirit of risk-taking. Safety is no bad thing. But if safety motivates your every action, you simply will find it impossible to embrace a biblical mindset oriented around strong manhood. To grow, you must risk. To lay hold of blessing, you must risk. To face down real foes, you must risk. To enter manhood, you must risk. To provide for your family, you must risk. There is no growth without risk. There is no dominion-taking without risk. Is it hard to adopt such a mentality when you have been steeped like tea in a culture of fearfulness? Yes, initially. But God blesses the enactment of biblical imperatives. As you pray to reject timidity and embrace a right vision of risk, God will work in you. God will make you a man.

Men Are Decisive

This element of manhood works hand-in-glove with the previous one. In order to take risks, you have to be able to make decisions. If you cannot make decisions, you will not be able to grow and mature. You will stay stuck. You will live in a kind of never-resolving gray mist, and you will find joy very hard to come by as a result. Your life will become one long spinning wheel, never at rest, never satisfied, never solid.

Men *must* make decisions. We see decisive leadership all throughout the Scriptures; we think of how elders, for example, are to "put what remains into order," an undertaking that depends upon decisiveness and clarity (Titus 1:5). To do so, of course, you must first have a backbone. You must be willing to get it wrong. In fact, you must not only be willing for this to happen, you must *know* that you will sometimes err. You must run this risk, and by God's grace, you must not allow yourself to become trapped by pressure to make the perfect decision (as discussed above). There simply is no way to mistake-proof your decisions.

Note that decisive men are hungry for wisdom and think deeply about their options. They pray much—but then they decide. They move ahead. They make a call. And when they do, they live with the consequences. Their mentality is not "get this one right or die," but more in the vein of "win or learn." If you get it right, great; if you get it wrong, learn from what you did, and keep going.

Men Talk Straight

Men should talk directly. I don't mean that in every conversation we should spew whatever comes into our mind; we all need to cultivate wise, gracious, and discrete speech. But the thoughtful man should have the ability to speak clearly. He should not hide his convictions behind qualifications, fancy words, or tangents. He should not speak elliptically. He should converse warmly, deeply, intelligently, interestingly, and with real clarity. Yet if he is asking you to do something, you should know what he wants you to do, why he wants you to do it, and how you can do it satisfactorily. Such speech represents an ordered mind, a present and engaged person, and a recognition of others' dignity.

It is not easy to train a young man to speak this way. A godly father draws his son out, encourages him to speak clearly, and gives him freedom to think out loud. He does not let his boy get lost in TechWorld, either: for considerable parts of the day, boys need to get off screens, off games, and be led into conversation. At dinnertime, they should converse with the rest of the family. When they're old enough, they should order their own food at restaurants. When an adult performs a service for them in a business or gym, they should thank that person.

If we would have our boys lead in the home, church, and society, then we must train them to communicate with clarity. Doing so takes work, but effectively represents a great gift to them—and to those they will lead. If a man is not willing to speak clearly, he is not ready to lead, because leadership depends upon clarity.

Men Pursue Discipline

The good life for a man is not a wild, out-of-control, binge-everything experience. The disciplined life is the good life. Being under control and under discipline is not weakness; it is strength that is rightly channeled and restrained. Self-rule powered by the grace of God is the ultimate freedom. It is greater than what you will find in any outlet, any other worldview, any other men's outreach. Christian freedom is true freedom; Christian discipline is true self-rule. The man who embraces self-rule by the power of God and to His glory is the man who is no longer in chains. Once enslaved to his lusts, desires, and wants, now he is a soldier under orders in the name of Christ. He is a man whose dignity and purpose are restored.

Such an existence carries with it challenges, difficulties, and frustrations. There is no way to pain-proof your sojourn on this earth. But the man who walks in these ways gets to taste many pleasures and joys. The disciplined life is the good life God wants for us men, and the one that yields much blessing for others. But not so the undisciplined. As Proverbs 25:28 reminds us, "A man without self-control is like a city broken into and left without walls." There are many wall-less men out there today; by God's grace, let us not be one of them. Let us be calm, controlled, upright, and disciplined.

Men Show Ferocity

As we have seen, men should not try to wipe out their God-given testosterone. We should wake up every day seeking to use our masculine capacities to serve God, bless our loved ones, and bring light to the darkness. This never means attacking innocent people. No, our capacity for fierceness, even ferocity, should come out in the face of evil and when great fortitude is needed for important tasks. We need to be men like John the Baptist, who confronted a pagan ruler for engaging in a sexual relationship with his brother's wife. John boldly and uncompromisingly told Herod of his sin, and as a result, Herod put him in prison and had him beheaded. John had a certain ferocity to him—not a hatred of his fellow man, mind you, but a hatred of evil. That hatred of evil compelled him to speak the truth in love (see Matthew 14:1–12).

This is the biblical pattern of strong men. They simply do not yield before towering evil and fearsome odds. We looked at some examples of such manhood in Chapter 4 and could add many more: Elijah facing down four hundred prophets of Baal (1 Kings 18), Daniel refusing to stop praying to the true God in Babylon (Daniel 1–2), Paul getting attacked but still going into synagogue after synagogue to proclaim Christ (Acts 18). None of these men hated flesh and blood; they hated Satan's work in God's world, and so they resolved to fight it to the bitter end. They fought it not weakly, but in God-given strength and resolve. So should we.

Men Are Rough

There is a roughness to manhood that is dying in our time. You see a certain texture to many male working environments. There is banter and good-natured ribbing; there is friendly-but-cutting humor and some sarcasm; there is a complex code of respect at work; there is a tendency toward understatement and an intentional withholding element that generates yet more banter; there is a willingness to do hard work; toughness is praised, and softness is derided, being self-focused and sharing too much personal information is discouraged.

In all this, you can find an element of roughness that is hard to pin down but is an innate part of masculine cultures. At its core, this is a resistance to softness. Men need such an instinct. We think of the shepherds of the Old Testament: David's ability to live in the wild and withstand hard challenges as a flock-herder prepared him for a greater calling (see 1 Samuel 16–17). Why does this matter for us? Because today, men are urged by many to be only tender when they need to also be tough. Roughness makes up part of this quality. We want to form men who fit in many different situations, who can be at home around many different types of people and endure hard situations. If all of life is easy and smooth, men lose something vital.

Men Are Kind

Though our culture pits strength against gentleness, in the Bible, no such tension exists. In the New Testament, the Christ who makes a whip of cords and scourges the moneychangers in the Temple is the same Christ who invites the little children to come to Him. In similar terms, the elder who must protect the flock is the same man who must not exasperate his children. Godly men are gentle and kind, even as they are tough and immovable (1 Corinthians 15:58).

Our world is crying out for kind men. We have opportunities all around us to show kindness. Some of these may yield Gospel witness, and some may not. When we see a neighborhood child, we can greet them. When a child holds a door open for us, we can thank them. When we're at a gathering and people around us feel awkward, we can try to make them feel comfortable. When we talk to women who are not our wives, we can be careful but friendly, and work to put them at ease. Men should be kind, and where we are not naturally, we should pray for God to grow us. Opting out of our culture's demand that we be *soft men* in no way means that we have a license to abandon the pursuit of the spiritual fruits of gentleness, kindness, and meekness (see Galatians 5:22–23).

Men Love Laughter

Godly men should be serious, but never cheerless. Though serious men, we should be the types who lift others up, not with artifice but with a smile, a wink, and a quick joke. We should tickle our children, enliven a gloomy workplace, and ambush a morose gathering with laughter. Our God is the God who gladdens hearts, after all. God gives "wine to gladden the heart of man, oil to make his face shine, and bread to strengthen man's heart" (Psalm 104:15). A glad heart produces joy, encouragement, good cheer, and laughter. We should not fear joy or distrust it; we should be marked by it.

Strong men should receive the pleasures of this life with an open hand and a grateful heart. Laughter, like all Gospel joy, is a protest against Satan's tyranny; it is a rebuke to perpetual bleakness of spirit; it is a sign of greater joy in the cosmos. Laughter signals that something has been loosed in this cursed realm, something wonderful and wild, something that the bureaucrats and thought police can neither apprehend nor tame. Men should be quick to joy, known to smile, and eager to laugh.

Men Cultivate Dignity

In an androgynous, gender-neutral order, there is no such thing as dignity. There is really only the effervescent virtue of "self-expression," which simultaneously means everything and nothing. In truth, men should cultivate dignity, as we see in different biblical examples. When Noah is drunk and uncovered in his tent, he compromises his standing as a father and a distinguished man of God (see Genesis 9). We should not aspire to the uncouthness of Noah; we should pursue something better.

As one application, we men should pursue looking distinguished in the right contexts. There is not one perfect masculine style. We have freedom in this regard, and many of us enjoy comfortable athletic wear. But even as we enjoy comfort, we should seek to look like adults. We may not always dress formally, but we should nonetheless cultivate an appropriate sense of dignity and masculine style. At least some of the time, we should dress up. Men should not be schlubs. As we have seen, men should look like men, and that calls for learning the ways of the gentleman. At minimum, we want to be men of dignity, men who treat others courteously, men who respect offices and institutions, and men who present themselves in a dignified way.

Men Sacrifice Themselves

We will give just one final word: Men must embrace self-sacrifice. As this book has argued repeatedly, the call of God on men to lead is neither a call to self-exaltation nor to self-preservation. The call to lead is in many ways the complete reverse of what the world thinks it is. As we have studied, in Ephesians 5:22–33, the Apostle Paul calls a husband to lay down his own interests for the good of his wife. This does not mean a man never has preferences, opinions, or desires—nor does it mean that he fails to lead, or only leads by doing what his wife would prefer. Doing so would be uncourageous and compromised; he must lead as he believes God would have him lead. It means that a godly man is always thinking of how he can strengthen and bless his wife.

This is what the example of Jesus Christ shows us. Leadership and authority went through a complete redefinition when Christ showed up on the scene. Though He is the one who hung all the stars and planets and is the only reason any person has breath in their lungs, Christ came not to be served but to serve (Matthew 20:28). In this way, He shows us that the world has things completely wrong. Titles are not important; humility is. Self-sacrifice thus is not a small or occasional component of our life; it is our life. Seen in this way, laying down our life is no burden to us. It is a privilege.

Conclusion

God made men in a distinctive way. Unlike our culture, which mocks this truth and tells men to be less like a natural man and more like a woman, the Bible celebrates manhood and trains men to embrace their God-given identities and instincts. In truth, they only rightly honor God when they love being a man and do all they can to *act like men* every minute of their existence.

In celebrating this truth, as we have in this chapter, we should not expect applause from the world. Satan has always hated God's design, and so hates manhood even as he hates womanhood. Satan wants to blur the lines between the sexes and ruin men. We must resist the devil's work in this regard. Whether we have a public platform to proclaim the distinctiveness of men or not, we should take joy in being men.

There is a way of life that God wants us to inhabit. We have captured some of this approach in this chapter, but manhood, in the final analysis, is not meant to be studied as a subject. Manhood is given to us by God to be lived to His glory.

In the broader war on men today, doing so in itself constitutes a victory.

CHAPTER 9

A Plan for Boys and a Way Back for Men

We don't need a containment strategy.
We need an annihilation strategy.

Former U.S. Defense Secretary Jim "Mad Dog" Mattis on ISIS

Some of the worst things happen when no one has a plan. Conversely, some of the best times emerge when someone forms a plan. This contrast is illustrated in a memorable way in a famous scene from the TV series *Band of Brothers*. Easy Company is called to rush toward Foy, a French town held by German forces, and take it. They advance rapidly despite a terrible artillery onslaught from the enemy. Just as they make it to the outskirts of the town, however, the entire advance halts. The commander in charge of the mission, long suspect for his poor leadership, suffers a breakdown. Several men get hurt and others killed because of his ineptitude.

When it appears that Easy Company will be blasted to pieces, a man named Lieutenant Speirs suddenly races across the battlefield. As calm as he is fast, Speirs turns the situation around. He quickly articulates a revised plan of attack, issues several orders, and rallies the men. At the same time, he braves enemy fire in almost foolhardy fashion. As a result of Speirs's direction and courage, the Allied forces take the town. Speirs had a plan, and his plan—backed by his courageous action—galvanized the flagging soldiers.

Watching that episode (one based on actual events), we are reminded of the need to formulate a structure for action. Like Speirs, we cannot just identify a broad goal; we have to spring into action. We need a plan. In fact, as Ryan Michler captures, this is the pathway to masculine satisfaction. We don't want to be ethereally "happy"; Michler contends that "we want to feel useful, productive, and valuable, or what I describe as *fulfilled*."[1] This fulfillment comes not from ease, usually, but from overcoming hardship. This is especially true when we recognize that fulfillment ultimately comes only from knowing God and pursuing His glory.

Toward that end, here are seven emphases ordered toward building strong men in a culture that has formally and informally declared war on them.

First, we need to call men to salvation.

We are all born weak and evil. We all need Christ. We all need redemption in His name by His blood. None of us has hope in ourselves; none of us can save ourselves. We cannot reclaim masculine practices, ways of thought, and disciplines and expect that we will be made whole by them alone. As fallen men, it is true that we have many needs in many directions, but our greatest need is God. Our greatest problem is our own sin, far more than any other factor affecting us; our perfect hope is Christ's own righteousness.

This conviction admittedly sets this book apart from many other resources on manhood. This does not mean that Christians alone can see truth in this realm; others also have access to God's common grace and self-revelation. But it does mean that this book—unlike resources that "hack" manhood, teach you genuinely valuable practices, and rightly call you to find dignity in your masculinity—cannot stop with the mere revival of manly thought and action. We need more horse-power than this—much more.

It is good to get stronger, become leaner, develop toughness, enact discipline, live out an authentic emotional life, and more. But none of these discoveries will save your soul; none of them will clear your guilt; none of them will result in a new nature within you. We are spiritual beings made by God so that we would everlastingly know God. Until we recover the means back to Him, we are merely putting Band-Aids on our souls, and they will not last long.

We men need salvation above all. All true and sound manhood flows from this spiritual miracle. A saved man is a strong man. By the Spirit's enabling, we now can truly "act like men" (1 Corinthians 16:13). Unsaved men can live out certain aspects and dimensions of manhood, but they cannot become strong men in God's sight without His work in them.

Second, we need to help men grow spiritually.

There are two dimensions to such growth. First, we need to cultivate a strong *private walk*. This means, in general and with some necessary flexibility baked in, a daily diet of Bible reading and prayer. For most of us, this means getting up earlier than we otherwise would. For perhaps twenty to thirty minutes (or longer), we read the Bible. I recommend reading a chapter or two in the Old Testament and a chapter or two in the New Testament each day. It is no bad thing to read from a study Bible, as the notes at the bottom of the page can lend discernment and understanding.

Men can also set a goal of praying for twenty to thirty minutes per day. There is freedom in how we do this; as a pretty active man who genuinely enjoys working out, I tend to pray while on the rowing machine, of all places. There is no perfect key to steadfast and unimpeded prayer, but taking walks can work well, or being in a quiet room without your phone or screens, or even praying as you commute back and forth to your job.

The goal is not for us to read Scripture and pray only at certain times. The goal is to establish a baseline of spiritual discipline. Once God builds this in your life, you'll actually find yourself with a greater hunger for spiritual growth. It's much like physical discipline: when you're not pursuing it, it's very hard to scrape together the will to start it, but when you start pursuing it, you find yourself with a growing capacity for more. Powered by the grace of God in you, you might start by forcing yourself to get in the Word and prayer, but as time goes on, you end up *wanting* to study and commune with God.

Second, we need to cultivate a strong *public walk*. By this I mean, quite simply, that men need the church. Too often, they get isolated. One of the best ways to work against this natural instinct is to join a church. But men should not linger on the periphery, either. We should jump in and find ways to serve the church. No form of service is too humble for us; in the Kingdom of Christ the Foot-Washer, all service unto God has meaning.

Boys should be raised in the church. This will shape them in many ways and counter some of their unhealthy tendencies as they grow up and make their own decisions. Instead of remaining loners, they can become members of the church. Instead of evading accountability, they can be known by the church community. Instead of seeking to be served, they can find ways to serve the congregation. Doing so will have a major effect on our sons and will help them understand that their lives are to be lived in community in appropriate ways.

My father loved our small local church, and it greatly impacted me. He made service to our small Baptist church in Maine a crucial aspect of his calendar. He loved it. He was there when the church doors were open. That had a real effect on me as his son. It showed me that Dad did not think that he was self-sufficient but recognized himself as a redeemed man in need of God's grace and the Word's teaching. We men need the church, and we need to hear God's call to it and bring others along with us as He allows.

Third, we need to ennoble men.

Contrary to the messages they receive regularly today, boys are not idiots. They are not something patriarchal to be "smashed." They are not inherently "toxic." Boys are made by God. At the creational level, God designed every aspect of boyhood and thus manhood. God did not make the woman and pronounce her "very good," only to make the man and pronounce him "pretty good." God made both sexes, investing them each with nothing less than divine significance and value. This includes men: men are noble, bearing great dignity and purpose.

In practical terms, we want to raise our boys to understand their God-given nobility. Here are some ways we can do this:

- Communicate to our boys that God has made them fearfully and wonderfully
- Teach them to conduct themselves like future men by doing things like standing up straight, looking people in the eye, shaking hands firmly, speaking politely to adults, and behaving well in group settings
- Regularly tell them that we love them and value them
- Praise them when they get things right and start showing their abilities and strengths
- Correct them when they get things wrong, doing so with firmness and self-control

- Take interest in what they are interested in, even as we encourage them to develop by directing them toward certain pursuits (sports, music, craftsmanship, technology, and more)

Ennobling boys is closely connected to loving them—and loving them is closely connected to paying attention to them. In a society that writes boys off, we need to love them, pay attention to them, and teach them that they have God-made dignity and purpose.

Fourth, we need to prepare our boys to work.

The duty of work is very close to the heartbeat of manhood. Men who are not working are men who are likely struggling. Men who are working are men who are, at least in a basic way, living out a key portion of their God-given identity. Men are made to be providers; men are made to be workers. Pastor Mike Fabarez says it well in his excellent book *Raising Men, Not Boys*:

> Our boys have been crafted by God to bring Him glory by exercising dominion over a segment of God's creation.... They will fill a role in this world as workers, spending more than half of their waking hours giving themselves to specific tasks, which not only earn them a paycheck but also bring honor to Christ.[2]

Well before our sons enter the workforce, we need to train them to work. This means that in the home, we partner them up with Dad to do tasks around the house. As they get older, they can take on bigger and more time-consuming jobs. By the time they are in high school, they should be ready and eager to work a part-time job or some approximation of the same. As we have noted, training boys to work is not an incidental part of their maturity; it is a major part of transition-ing them to adulthood. Nothing so emancipates a young man as when he earns his own money, buys his own possessions (at least some of them), and keeps his own hours (to a degree). It is not an exaggeration to say that training boys to work readies boys for manhood.

On the other hand, if we rob boys of this opportunity, we stunt them. They will not grow. They will not mature. They will not take responsibility for themselves the way they would otherwise. We live in a culture that offers boys the easy way out: they need not show up, they need not prepare themselves, they need not take themselves seriously, and they can simply ease back and live life through screens. This is a recipe for disaster, and many are following it today. As a result, young men languish.

Entering the work world is often challenging and even harsh; it forces you outside of yourself. If you work, say, at an auto parts store, you have to engage customers, communicate clearly, show up on time, work late, do things that weren't initially asked of you, and handle things like a man. This is a big reason why work is so important for young men: it draws out of them skills and traits that otherwise lie dormant. Here are a few practical steps to consider along these lines:

- Boys need to be given household tasks or chores on a regular basis
- Work should be done cheerfully and satisfactorily
- When possible, fathers should work with their boys, giving them an example to follow
- Boys should get a job when it is appropriate for them to do so
- Whether entering the workforce or going to college after high school, boys should have a plan to save money and avoid debt (or have a plan to pay it off)

Of course, each family has its own situation. There is not one perfect way to train boys to work. Whatever precise path we use to get our boys ready, the point stands: we need to get them ready and help them live out a vital part of who God made them to be.

Fifth, boys need to be trained to honor women.

As in so many areas, this starts in the home. Boys must honor their mothers. This is established by a father who models such conduct. He does not belittle his wife but speaks well of her. He does not begrudge his wife's needs and requests but loves and cherishes her. He does not leave his wife to fend for herself but strives to strengthen her any way he can.

When a marriage has this grace-powered dynamic, a son is set up to understand that women deserve loving honor. The same holds true with his sisters. He will have his own relationship with them, but he does not treat them like his brothers or his friends. He treats them with dignity: he holds doors for them, carries in groceries for them, shovels the sidewalk for them, locks the doors at night when Dad is away, and generally seeks to be strong for them in a loving way.

Boys should honor women but not fear them. They need training to be able to talk to girls in a respectful yet engaging way. As they become young men, they need help to steer clear of goofy machismo on the one hand and terrified timidity on the other. Young men should confidently but humbly approach young women, treating them well. They should be able to hold a conversation with them and to respect them as people, not see them as merely objects of romantic interest. Young men should be trained to be kind to all girls, not merely the pretty or vivacious ones. They should do in public what they do in the home, and hold doors for women, pick up the chairs after the youth group Bible study, volunteer to pray at the end of a group event, and generally do whatever they can to honor women.

Some men are called to be single; most are called to marry. Both callings can honor the Lord. Whatever the Lord has in store for our sons, we want to train them from their earliest days to honor women and treat them well. Doing so when they are young will help them greatly when they are older.

Sixth, boys should cultivate manliness and feel no shame for it.

Too many boys and young men feel tentative in their own skin today. They know what *not* to do, having heard too many boy-directed rules and directives to count in their young lives, but they do not necessarily know what *to* do, for many of them have had little training, discipleship, or investment.

They have certain instincts, appetites, emotions, abilities, proclivities, and interests, but they have been told over and over again that boys and girls are basically the same. Further, they have heard it repeated many times that *anything boys can do, girls can do better.* Said on the playground, this is harmless; said by a parent or educator, and this can do damage. In similar terms, when boys have acted in boyish ways, they have sometimes been taken to task severely. Many of these boys know they don't quite fit into their surroundings, but they do not know why or what to do about this perplexing situation.

We cannot fix our culture in one fell swoop. But here is what we can do: we can encourage young men to be distinctly boyish and manly. This starts in the context of a healthy family. God intends that manhood would be both displayed and taught by a father to his son. He wants boys to smell what men smell like. He wants boys to trail their fathers around the house, asking them questions and watching them fix things (or trying to, in my case). He wants boys to be disciplined by fathers with firmness but also loving control. He wants boys to watch as Dad walks over to Mom, whispers in her ear, and pulls her close for a quick kiss. Manhood is taught, yes, but it also is meant to be lived, displayed, and caught.

We need to consider practical ways that we can cultivate manliness in our boys. Or, if you're a grown man trying to figure out what manliness looks like, here are some practical suggestions:

- Recognize in fundamental terms that God made you a man for His glory
- Try to grow a beard to see if you like this distinctive physical feature of manhood
- Get in shape, and change your body from a liability into a weapon
- Develop your shoulders, and eat enough food to keep you from being emaciated
- Deepen your voice by speaking from your stomach cavity, not your throat
- Push your shoulders back, and stand with your chest out; look people in the eye when you talk, and hold their gaze
- Don't endlessly qualify yourself when you talk; speak clearly and unapologetically, while mixing in humor, humility, and a dose of self-deprecation
- When with other people, hold some part of yourself in reserve; don't be a motormouth, saying anything that comes to mind
- Show emotion at appropriate times, whether joy or grief or consternation, but avoid being an emotional fountain
- Give your wife space to be the woman in the relationship; men should not cry more than women, but should be their wife's rock

- Get outside and do challenging physical things from time to time
- Get a good haircut that fits your frame (goodbye to the man-bun and accompanying scrunchie); in general, take care of yourself and present yourself well
- Buy some good cologne and wear a non-suffocating amount of it
- Show up on time, ready to go and ready to work
- If you lead meetings or services, lead them with poise and confidence, and don't be afraid to move things ahead, make clear decisions, and build camaraderie
- Be polite, kind, and gentle, but don't be a pushover
- When confrontation or conflicts arise, choose to sort things out directly rather than passive-aggressively, and be ready to detail what you did wrong whenever applicable

The foregoing practices—in general terms—used to be handed down generationally. This has changed today, as fatherlessness and a hostile culture have led to the loss of much practical guidance on manhood. We cannot let such a vacuum endure. We who love boys and young men need to help them understand not only the theology of manhood, but the practice of it.

In stating this, we also recognize freedom and flexibility in numerous aspects of our embodiment of manhood. Much of the foregoing suggestions involve wisdom; we're not handing down a new tablet of commandments that we have created from on high. Nonetheless, this truth stands: we men should joyfully seek to live distinctively as males, and we need to clarify what that looks like for the rising generation.

This last comment matters greatly. Whatever precise choices we make regarding our masculine appearance and behavior, our practice is always driven by the biblical text. The Scripture does not blur the line between the sexes; it draws the line between them as a positive good. As we saw in Chapter 6, God wants men to look like men and women to look like women. Our androgynous culture militates against sexual distinctiveness, but God loves it and calls for it as a matter of Christian faithfulness.

This means that we should aim to display the unique goodness of manhood in the body God has given us. We have freedom here in many respects; all cultures are not the same, to say the very least. But the charge to embody our God-given sex as a matter of worship cuts across all cultures and sets the mark for us. In a gender-neutral and androgyny-celebrating age, we have a great opportunity to exhibit the distinctive goodness of manhood.

Our stylistic choices and preferences will vary, but strong men will collectively take joy both in being and being perceived to be men. This is not due to insecurity, fear, or foolishness. This is due to our gratitude to God for being made men and our eagerness to live out our masculine identity in a way that brings God all the glory we can.[3] Doing so, furthermore, is a matter of Christian witness. As we saw earlier, ancient Corinth was deeply pagan, and it was that church that Paul exhorted to display distinctive manhood and womanhood. Doing so glorifies God and is also evangelistic, setting the cross-purchased Church apart from the creature-worshiping culture.

Manhood is spiritual at its core, absolutely. But if God wanted us men to be Gnostic spirits, hovering over the ground like a halo, He would have formed us that way. Physicality matters. The body matters. Our appearance matters. In sum, the point stands: we should cultivate manliness, and feel no shame over doing so.

Seventh, men need to confess, repent, and turn from sin when they fail.

Though it may sound defeatist to some, this is a very important matter. Ironically, if we set the standard unrealistically and expect perfection from men, we will only encourage them to sin. They will either grow proud, pretend they do not really sin, or get deeply discouraged as honesty reveals the disparity between conduct and standard. Let us break down how these responses could manifest in men:

Pride: Men could fall into the pharisaical trap of thinking they really are above other people, and that they basically do not sin in any meaningful way. This goes against the Scripture, which teaches that we "all stumble in many ways" (James 3:2). Pride is deadly and will spread through a man like cancer, corrupting him.

Pretending: Men might know they sin, but minimize it. When confronted, they might deflect, blame others, offer excuses, and fight off the conviction of sin. Note that this too is pride, but in a different form.

Depressed: Men might know all too well that they sin, and having sought an unrealistic goal, might thus give up and get discouraged without relief. Instead of handling sin and failing honestly and maturely as we should, they might see sin as huge and grace as small, when for the believer, the reverse is true: grace is huge and sin gets conquered by it.

Men of all sin patterns need God inexhaustibly. There is never a day of our existence in which we do not need to depend wholly upon the Lord. There is not a day in which we should not pursue growth in godliness in all facets of our life. Even when we are born again, we always need Jesus. We always need Christ to go before us, forgive our daily sins and failings, and remake us into His perfect image. No man is self-sufficient. None of us can keep ourselves in the faith by our own strength. God has made us strong in Christ, but we are always the weak partner in the venture.

Men who may have experienced significant brokenness in the distant or recent past (or the present) need to hear this message. This is the heart of Christianity. God saves us and matures us, but He also deals with us over the long haul. When our sin patterns yield real effects and broken relationships, we must not forget that God's grace goes with us into the valley of darkness. When Christ is our savior, God is with us in the shadows; He is with us in the low places, and He is with us as we survey the wreckage of our life and mourn it.

All this is due to the doctrine of what is called "union with Christ." This means that there is never a time as a believer when you are not "in Christ" by faith and Christ is not in you by faith. The Apostle Paul expresses this doctrine when he writes,

> To them God chose to make known how great among the
> Gentiles are the riches of the glory of this mystery, which is
> *Christ in you*, the hope of glory. (Colossians 1:27, emphasis
> mine)

What a wonder, and what a comfort! Christ is not only with us, but in us as believers. He is with us and in us as we try to make sense of bewildering circumstances and fresh challenges: Divorce. Death. Estrangement. Conflict. Embitterment. Unmet expectations. Fractured love. Abandonment. Physical pain. Sleeplessness. Unrelenting stress. The burden of caring for family or friends. Never measuring up. Never knowing your father. Never connecting with your mother. Never being discipled. Never being trained. Only rarely hearing "I love you." Christ is with us and in us as we grapple with all of these things and more.

This is not an easy world. It is not a soft place, and it is not made for soft men. Were it not for the love of God, we would surely be overcome by the waves of suffering and sin that buffet all of us. Perhaps you have even experienced this; perhaps your sin has taken you far from shore, far from solidity and strength. If that is true, hear once more the amazing news of Christianity: Jesus Christ is a rescue swimmer. He can go into the deepest depths.

Through the cross, Jesus takes us out of the watery grave, but not before He leaves our sin there, never to be found, never to be held to our account again. He buries our sin and resurrects our souls. He does this by His atoning death on the cross; in dying in our place, He drank the Father's just wrath against our sin and enabled us to go free. But the good news does not stop there: Jesus was raised to life by the Father. He is the resurrection, and He loves to wash the sins of the guilty, give them saving faith, and so bring us to life.

This is the good news of the Gospel. It is good news when we are saved, and it is good news all the days of our life. That is why we started this practical section with a focus on salvation, and why we end it with a focus on salvation. We always need God's grace and God's power. Praise God, we have it. When we sin, when we stumble, when our patterns of wrongdoing are revealed, forgiveness holds. Redemption does not blink out. The servers of divine love never melt. The blood of Christ never loses its power.

Unlike so many other systems and religions, Christianity does not ask that you clean yourself up before you come in the Father's house. You come, as the great old hymn says, *just as you are.* You come broken by sin and ruined by pride. You come, brokenhearted, and see that God is there, waiting for you. You come, downcast, and find that the door is not locked, but open wide. All the lights in the house are on, and there is a welcoming party thrown in your honor. You come, a prodigal, and see your heavenly Father not merely willing to receive you, but running toward you, so eager is He to forgive you (Luke 15:11–32).

The Yearning for a Higher Call

Men who have failed and flamed out need these words. Men struggling against the war being waged against them need them as well. Men are not "toxic." They are sinners like women, and like women, they need the grace of God. Men are not idiots; they are not outmoded; they should not stop striving to be and act like men. Nor is the future female, with men out of the picture. Men do not need cancellation, hatred, or "smashing," whatever that means. Men need God. Men need grace. Men need a call to leave sin behind and trust Christ.

It is time for such a restoration. It is time for men to rise once more. Men are longing for such a call to stand up and be counted. We men may be flagging today, but we nonetheless yearn for a summons to a greater cause than our own self-gratification and a greater mission than the perpetuation of our own comfort. Joining a greater work will cost us, we know; enlisting in a greater force may well take us to the very end of ourselves. But still the urge to find such an endeavor, something much bigger than us, persists. In fact, the costliness of the great call to battle strangely makes it all the more appealing.

Here is the truth: we are in fact at war. The great campaign we seek is right in front of us, even if it is often invisible. As he did long ago, the evil adversary still battles to take men—called by God to leadership in home, church, and society—down. The antichrist spirit speaks through many outlets and individuals today, demanding that men lean back, that they accept the truth of their inherent "toxicity," that they embrace low expectations and abandon their innate aggressiveness. Tragically, many men comply. Once, they had a role to play; once, they were daring and bold; once, they sought to embody authority in love. But no longer. Now, men must predominantly become *soft men*.

Not all will do so, however. Some will disappear, becoming *lost men*. Others will reject the terms of woke feminism, but foolishly become *exaggerated men*, gratifying their flesh and living for themselves. Still others will become *angry men* and lash out at the world as it has come to them, inflicting violence and death on the defenseless. Few will take note of them until it is too late—and then, the same public order that has problematized manhood will wring its hands at this most recent outbreak.

But all is not lost. There is another group of men who will not go soft. They will not disappear. They will not puff out their chest and live by the flesh. They will not attack the innocent and vent their rage. They will hear the serpent's whisper to walk in these ways, but by the grace of God, they will reject the snake's hiss. They will hear and answer a higher call, the call of Christ to all sinners—men and women alike—to repent of their sin, trust the crucified and resurrected God-man, and live by faith. These men will become the fifth type of man found in Scripture: they will become, against all the odds, *strong men*.

Conclusion

There are no strong men in natural terms, truly. But thankfully, there are weak men made strong by God. In evil and low days like ours, we need just this kind of man. This is not a luxury item added to the cart; strong manhood powered by the grace of God is the greatest anthropological need we have. As I have labored to establish throughout this book, if we form strong men, we will form strong marriages. If we form strong marriages, we will build strong churches.

If we build strong churches, we will contribute to strong communities. If we have strong communities and strong men acting in public for the good of others, God will get much glory, and people will flourish.

But achieving this end is no easy accomplishment. We are indeed in war. Men are considered "toxic" by many. In a hostile climate, boys are struggling; young men are failing; adult men are languishing. Strong manhood has many enemies, and they will only grow in number as time goes on. But here is the good news: God loves strong manhood. Even if a strong man stands alone for what is true and right and good, he may know that God is with him and the smile of God is upon him.

Men are not toxic. Men are not outmoded. In the war on men that rages today, we hear these lies. We hear it said in various ways that strong men are the problem. But this is not true. Though men are under severe fire today, we will not be silent. We will confess this without blinking and without flinching: powered by the grace of God, strong men are the *solution*.

Acknowledgments

This project is dedicated to a man made strong by God, Grant Castleberry. For over a decade now, Grant has been a dear friend, brother-at-arms, colaborer, counselor, and blessing to me. In my years knowing Grant, I can truly say that a friend sticks closer than a brother. God was kind to give me Grant as a best friend. This began in our years of service with the Council on Biblical Manhood and Womanhood, and will endure amidst many trials—I pray—until the Lord takes us off the field.

Great thanks go to Tim Peterson for acquiring this book and seeing the vision for it, and to Julie Jayne for heading up Salem Books with grace and class. How thankful I am that Salem Books is not only willing to tackle hot-button subjects, but glad to do so in order to strengthen many. A rare publisher, this. I am grateful as well to Voddie Baucham Jr. for writing such a wise and galvanizing foreword. Voddie is serving well in the Lord's army, and I give thanks to God for his friendship and inspiration. My gratitude as well to Karla Dial for her expert editing and help along the way, as with Jennifer Valk and the rest of the Salem team.

A warm word of appreciation for my colleagues at Grace Bible Theological Seminary, and I thank the board and President Jeff

185

Johnson for the space given me to write. How I appreciate the encouraging saints at Grace Bible Church as well. My thanks for their prayers and kind words during the writing of this book.

My lovely wife, Bethany, has supported me all through this project with good cheer, great advice, and feminine kindness. I love being her husband, and I love our three children with all I have. These four know that I am not the man that I should be, but that by the grace of God, I will grow to be more like the true man, Jesus Christ, as the years go on.

My own father, Andrew Strachan, did much to model persevering and patient Christian manhood, and I find myself drawing on his lessons often—even as I give thanks to God for my loving and devoted mother and my little sister (intrepid in every way). Men are shaped in formative ways by fathers, but mothers play a big role, too, as do siblings.

Over the years, I have gleaned a harvest of wisdom from my father-in-law, Bruce Ware, an excellent husband, father, theologian, and churchman. How kind the Lord was to give me Dr. Ware as a sage guide! My grandfather, Daniel Dustin, was also a steady and loving influence on me; how I wish I could thank him face to face for his kindness. Soon, in eternal glory, I will. How thankful I am for these men and many more who have invested in me. My cup overflows.

In closing, I give thanks to the Trinitarian God of Scripture for the opportunity to write this book. The Father is a Father beyond compare; the Son is the Savior of my soul; the Holy Spirit makes me strong in grace.

Glory be to the Father, Son, and Spirit.

Amen.

Select References

Chanski, Mark. *Manly Dominion*. Amityville, New York: Calvary Press, 2007.

Esolen, Anthony. *No Apologies: Why Civilization Depends on the Strength of Men*. Washington, D.C.: Regnery Gateway, 2022.

Foster, Michael and Dominic Bnonn Tennant. *It's Good to Be a Man*. Moscow, Idaho: Canon Press, 2022.

Gurian, Michael. *The Wonder of Boys*. New York: Jeremy P. Tarcher/Putnam, 2006.

Hymowitz, Kay. *Manning Up*. New York: Basic Books, 2012.

Mansfield, Harvey. *Manliness*. New Haven, Connecticut: Yale University Press, 2007.

Peterson, Jordan. *12 Rules for Life*. Random House Canada, 2018.

Piper, John and Wayne Grudem, eds. *Recovering Biblical Manhood and Womanhood*. Wheaton, Illinois: Crossway, 2021.

Wilson, Douglas. *Future Men*. Moscow, Idaho: Canon Press, 2016.

Notes

Introduction

1. By "pagan," I do not merely mean "non-Christian ideology with which I do not agree." I mean this: "Paganism is the antiwisdom of the serpent which deconstructs ordered reality—the God-made world—and replaces it with a new order, an antiorder ruled by the devil. In this antiorder, there is no Creator; no divine design; no male or female; no script for sexuality; no God-designed family with a father, mother, and children; no need to protect and care for children at all; no Savior, Lord, or theistic end to the cosmos; and no judge of evil." Owen Strachan, *Reenchanting Humanity: A Theology of Mankind* (Fearn, Ross-Shire: Mentor, 2019), 200–202. This system follows "oneism" according to theologian Peter Jones, the view that everything is one, which contrasts with "twoism" per Christianity, which teaches that there is Creator and creation. To learn more, see Peter Jones, *Pagans in the Pews: How the New Spirituality Is Invading Your Home, Church, and Community* (Ventura, California: Regal, 2001). Jones saw this evil movement coming long before most anyone else did, but few heard him or paid attention.

2. Harvey Mansfield, *Manliness* (New Haven, Connecticut: Yale University Press, 2006), 23. I will cover the phenomenon of Jordan Peterson in Chapter 8, but it is worth noting that Mansfield represents a kind of proto-Peterson. His book and lectures on the subject of manhood ignited a firestorm rarely eclipsed by a public intellectual in the last one hundred years of Western life. Watching and learning from Mansfield almost twenty years ago, fresh out of Bowdoin College, I saw the kind of tempest that would arise in the wake of a strong assertion of manhood. Nonetheless, though not Christian in nature, Mansfield's work should be considered both brave and pioneering, much like Peterson's.

3. Joyce Carol Oates, (@JoyceCarolOates), "category of straight white males is the only category…," Twitter, October 19, 2022, 10:14 p.m., https://twitter.com/JoyceCarolOates/status/1582918080769900544.

4. Soumyabrata Gupta, "Avatar Director James Cameron Says Testosterone Is Toxic. 'Masculine' Twitter Calls Him 'Beta Male,'" Times Now, December

5, 2022, https://www.timesnownews.com/entertainment-news/avatar
-director-james-cameron-says-testosterone-is-toxic-masculine-twitter-calls
-him-beta-male-article-96001279.

5. Owen Daugherty, "'Traditional Masculinity' Deemed 'Harmful' by the
American Psychological Association," *The Hill*, January 10, 2019, https://
thehill.com/blogs/blog-briefing-room/news/424829-traditional
masculinity-deemed-harmful-by-american.

6. Ibid.

7. Ibid.

8. Richard Reeves, *Of Boys and Men: Why the Modern Male Is Struggling,
Why It Matters, and What to Do about It* (Washington, D.C.: Brookings,
2022), 36.

9. This book is all about men, but I could write a companion volume entitled
The War on Women, and it would be eminently justified (and needed).
Feminism, as Chapter 2 will show, has devastated modern womanhood,
as has sexual paganism more broadly. For now, my book *Reenchanting
Humanity* will have to suffice on this count; see Strachan, *Reenchanting
Humanity*, 141–47.

Chapter 1: How Men Are Struggling

1. Paulose Mar Paulose, "Encounter in Humanization: Insights for Christian-
Marxist Dialogue and Cooperation," Religion Online, https://www.religion
-online.org/book-chapter/chapter-4-marxs-critique-of-religion.

2. Isaiah Berlin, *Karl Marx: His Life and Environment*, 4th ed. (New York:
Oxford University Press, 1996), 19–20.

3. Steve Murch, "We Need to Talk about a Crisis for Young American Men,"
Post Alley, April 5, 2022, https://www.postalley.org/2022/04/05/we-need-to
-talk-about-a-crisis-for-young-american-men.

4. Philip Zimbardo, "Young Men and Society: We Will Only Get Out What
We Put In," Institute for Family Studies, January 14, 2021, https://ifstudies
.org/blog/young-men-and-society-we-will-only-get-out-what-we-put-in.

5. Ibid.

6. Nicholas Eberstadt, *Men Without Work: Post-Pandemic Edition* (West
Conshohocken, Pennsylvania: Templeton Press, 2022), 7.

7. Ibid., 3, 5.

8. Richard V. Reeves and Ember Smith, "The Male College Crisis Is Not Just
in Enrollment, but Completion," The Brookings Institution, October 8, 2021,

https://www.brookings.edu/blog/up-front/2021/10/08/the-male-college
-crisis-is-not-just-in-enrollment-but-completion.

9. Ibid.

10. Jon Marcus, "The Pandemic Is Speeding Up the Mass Disappearance of Men from College," The Hechinger Report, January 19, 2021, https:// hechingerreport.org/the-pandemic-is-speeding-up-the-mass-disappearance -of-men-from-college.

11. Zimbardo, "Young Men and Society."

12. Ibid.

13. Ibid.

14. Murch, "We Need to Talk about a Crisis for Young American Men."

15. "Porn Addiction Statistics," Guy Stuff Counseling and Coaching, https:// www.guystuffcounseling.com/porn-addiction-statistics.

16. "Internet Pornography by the Numbers: A Significant Threat to Society," Webroot, https://www.webroot.com/us/en/resources/tips-articles/internet -pornography-by-the-numbers.

17. Kirsten Weir, "Is Pornography Addictive?," *Monitor on Psychology* 45, no. 4 (April 2014): 46, https://www.apa.org/monitor/2014/04/pornography.

18. Julia DeCelles-Zwerneman, "Where Are All the Men? Exploring the Gender Gap in Church," Capterra, August 10, 2016, https://www.capterra .com/resources/where-are-all-the-men-exploring-the-gender-gap-in -church.

19. "Why Men Matter, Both Now and Forever," Washington Area Coalition of Men's Ministries, http://www.wacmm.org/Stats.html.

20. David French, "Men Are Getting Weaker—Because We're Not Raising Men," *National Review*, August 16, 2016, https://www.nationalreview .com/2016/08/male-physical-decline-masculinity-threatened.

21. Nancy Shute, "Kids Are Less Fit Today than You Were Back Then," NPR, November 20, 2013, https://www.npr.org/sections/health-shots/2013/11 /20/246316731/kids-are-less-fit-today-than-you-were-back-then.

22. "Body positivity" may seem right, and indeed we should steer clear of an unhealthy obsession with physical frame and performance. But body positivity bodes ill for the populace that embraces it. Better to practice a biblical concept, that of stewardship and dominion of the body by the power of God for the glory of God. That will direct us away from an ungodly physical focus while pushing us to honor God's gift of a body.

23. Neil Howe, "You're Not the Man Your Father Was," *Forbes*, October 5, 2017, https://www.forbes.com/sites/neilhowe/2017/10/02/youre-not-the -man-your-father-was/?sh=6519feed8b7f.

24. Saul Elbein, "Male Fertility Crash Accelerating Worldwide: Study," *The Hill*, November 15, 2022, https://thehill.com/policy/equilibrium-sustain ability/3736984-male-fertility-crash-accelerating-worldwide-study.

25. "Who Commits Crime?," *Social Problems: Continuity and Change*, University of Minnesota, https://open.lib.umn.edu/socialproblems/chapter /8-3-who-commits-crime/.

26. Derek Thompson, "Colleges Have a Guy Problem," *The Atlantic*, September 14, 2021, https://www.theatlantic.com/ideas/archive/2021/09/ young-men-college-decline-gender-gap-higher-education/620066.

27. Ibid.; The paper cited by Thompson is Raj Chetty et al., "Race and Economic Opportunity in the United States: An Intergenerational Perspective," Opportunity Insights, March 2018, http://www.equality-of -opportunity.org/assets/documents/race_paper.pdf.

28. U.S. Census Bureau, "Living Arrangements of Children Under 18 Years Old: 1960 to Present," U.S. Census Bureau, July 1, 2012, cited in "The Consequences of Fatherlessness," Fathers.com, https://fathers.com/the -consequences-of-fatherlessness.

29. U.S. Census Bureau, "America's Family and Living Arrangements: 2011, Table C8," Washington D.C., 2011.

30. U.S. Department of Health and Human Services, "Survey on Child Health," National Center for Health Statistics, Washington, D.C., 1993.

31. Heather A. Turner, David Finkelhor, and Richard Ormrod, "The Effect of Lifetime Victimization on the Mental Health of Children and Adolescents," *Social Science & Medicine* 62, no. 1 (January 2006): 13–27, https://doi.org /10.1016/j.socscimed.2005.05.03.

32. Warren Farrell, "Mass Shootings Are Part of Society's Boy Crisis," *New York Daily News*, June 6, 2022, https://www.nydailynews.com/opinion /ny-oped-mass-shootings-are-inseparable-from-our-boy-crisis-20220606 -3v27opdsfffwvde5eni6usn32y-story.html.

33. Anne-Marie Crowhurts, "Smash the Patriarchy," *CAM*, University of Cambridge, April 1, 2018, https://magazine.alumni.cam.ac.uk/patriarchy.

34. Ibid.

35. "SMASH the Patriarchy," ACLU of Oklahoma, June 16, 2022, https:// www.acluok.org/en/events/smash-patriarchy.

36. "Unlearning Toxic Masculinity," Brown University, https://www.brown .edu/campus-life/health/services/promotion/general-health-social-wellbeing -sexual-assault-dating-violence-get-involved-prevention/unlearning.

37. Ibid.; The article cites Peter Baker et al., "The Men's Health Gap: Men Must Be Included in the Global Health Equity Agenda," *Bulletin of the World Health Organization* 92, no. 8 (August 2014): 618–20, https://www .ncbi.nlm.nih.gov/pmc/articles/PMC4147416/pdf/BLT.13.132795.pdf.

38. Adam Gallie, "What Are the Top 10 Toxic Masculinity Behaviors?," New Dawn Aurora, July 23, 2019, https://www.aurorand.org.uk/news/top-10 -toxic-masculinity-behaviours.

39. Katie Mettler, "Hillary Clinton Just Said It, but 'the Future Is Female' Began as a 1970s Lesbian Separatist Slogan," *The Washington Post,* February 8, 2017, https://www.washingtonpost.com/news/morning-mix /wp/2017/02/08/hillary-clinton-just-said-it-but-the-future-is-female-began -as-a-1970s-lesbian-separatist-slogan.

40. Madame Gandhi, "The Future Is Female," *Madame Gandhi* (blog), https:// madamegandhi.blog/the-future-is-female.

41. Ibid.

42. Wildfang, "The Future Is Fluid—Tegan and Sara x Wildfang," YouTube, October 3, 2017, https://www.youtube.com/watch?v=IokNNQm4sKg.

Chapter 2: Why Men Are Struggling

1. Karl Marx and Frederick Engels, *The Communist Manifesto* (New York: International Publishers, 2020 [1848]), 26–27.

2. Frederick R. Smith, "Weird Wilhelm Reich," Frederick R. Smith Speaks, November 8, 2020, https://frederickrsmith.substack.com/p/weird -wilhelm-reich-20-11-09?utm_source=substack&utm_medium=email& utm_content=share.

3. This language is no longer used on the Black Lives Matter site. See Joshua Rhett Miller, "BLM Site Removes Page on 'Nuclear Family Structure' amid NFL Vet's Criticism," *New York Post,* September 24, 2020, https://nypost .com/2020/09/24/blm-removes-website-language-blasting-nuclear- family-structure/.

4. Simone de Beauvoir, *The Second Sex* (Paris: Gallimard, 1949), 267.

5. Linda Gordon, "Functions of the Family," *Women: A Journal of Liberation* 1, no. 2 (Fall 1969), 23. The quote continues: "Furthermore, this process must precede as well as follow the overthrow of capitalism, for unless some brave souls develop new living patterns now, the pressures towards

retrenchment that seem to follow most revolutions may stifle our advance"
(23). As is so often the case, attempts to destroy the family go hand-in-glove
with attempts to destroy the free market.

6. Robin Morgan, ed., *Sisterhood Is Powerful: An Anthology of Writings
    from the Women's Liberation Movement* (New York: Random House,
    1970), 537. For a brief treatment of Morgan's view that also features some
    of the voices quoted in this section, see Patrick Fagan and Lauren Noyes,
    "Why Congress Should Ignore Radical Feminist Opposition to Marriage,"
    The Heritage Foundation, June 16, 2003, https://www.heritage.org/welfare
    /report/why-congress-should-ignore-radical-feminist-opposition-marriage
    -0.

7. Nancy Lehmann and Helen Sullinger, *The Document: Declaration of
    Feminism* (1971), 11–12.

8. Robin Morgan, *Going Too Far: The Personal Chronicle of a Feminist*
    (New York: Vintage, 1978), 178.

9. Andrea Dworkin, *Intercourse* (New York: Free Press, 1987), 137.

10. Andrea Dworkin, *Our Blood: Prophecies and Discourses on Sexual
    Politics* (New York: Harper and Row, 1976), 20.

11. Susan Bridle, "No Man's Land: An Interview with Mary Daly,"
    EnlightenNext 16 (Fall–Winter 1999); interview accessed at https://
    www.yumpu.com/en/document/read/27846873/no-mans-land
    -ressourcesfeministes (the quote cited came on page 10 of this document,
    which runs 11 pages total).

12. Judith Butler, "Performative Acts and Gender Constitution: An Essay in
    Phenomenology and Feminist Theory," *Theatre Journal* 40, no. 4
    (December 1988): 520, https://doi.org/10.2307/3207893.

13. Ibid., 528.

14. Ibid.

15. C. S. Lewis, *The Abolition of Man* (New York: HarperCollins, 2001
    [1944]), 23.

16. Kay Hymowitz, *Manning Up: How the Rise of Women Has Turned Men
    into Boys* (New York: Basic Books, 2011), 71.

17. Debra Soh, *The End of Gender: Debunking the Myths about Sex and
    Identity in Our Society* (New York: Threshold Editions, 2020), 163.

18. Hanna Rosin, *The End of Men: And the Rise of Women* (New York:
    Riverhead Books, 2012), 11.

19. Ibid., 21.

20. Ibid., 267.

21. Mary Daly, *Beyond God the Father: Toward a Philosophy of Women's Liberation* (Boston: Beacon Press, 1993), 19; See Douglas F. Huffman and Eric L. Johnson, eds., *God Under Fire: Modern Scholarship Reinvents God* (Grand Rapids, Michigan: Zondervan, 2002), 264.

22. Mary Daly, *Amazon Grace: Re-Calling the Courage to Sin Big* (London: Palgrave MacMillan, 2006), 20–21. For insightful discussion of this quotation, see "Handout: Feminism of Daly and Ruether," Philosophical Investigations, March 3, 2018, https://peped.org/philosophicalinvestigations /handout-feminism-daly-ruether.

23. Rosemary Radford Ruether, *Women-Church: Theology and Practice of Feminist Liturgical Communities* (San Francisco: Harper and Row, 1985), 72.

24. William Hamilton, "In Piam Memoriam: The Death of God after Ten Years," *The Christian Century*, October 8, 1975, 872–73.

25. For some context, see Ayslin Rice, "Divine Feminine," Herchurch SF, October 15 (no year given), https://www.herchurch.org/about/divine -feminine.

26. See Miriam Therese Winter, "Our Mother Who Is within Us," *A Seat at the Table* (blog), February 24, 2010, http://acatholicwomansplace. blogspot.com/2010/02/our-mother-who-is-within-us.html.

27. Dan Skogen, "Worship of 'Goddess' in the ELCA and Led by Synod Council Leader," Exposing the ELCA, May 19, 2010, https://www .exposingtheelca.com/exposed-blog/worship-of-goddess-in-the-elca-and -lead-by-synod-council-leader.

28. "GenderBread Person v4.0," https://www.genderbread.org.

29. Trish Bendix, "What 'the Future Is Female' Really Means," Logo TV, October 19, 2017, https://www.logotv.com/news/z65pjw/tegan-and-sara -wildfang-the-future-is-fluid.

30. "BLACK LIVES MATTER: What We Believe," https://uca.edu/training /files/2020/09/black-Lives-Matter-Handout.pdf. Note: this webpage has been taken down during the course of writing this book.

31. Ibid.

32. Irving Kristol, "The Adversary Culture of Intellectuals," *Encounter*, October 1979, 6.

Chapter 3: The Foundation of Strong Manhood: Genesis 1–3

1. Staff Report, "Ascension Parish Deputy Nominated for Valor Award," *Gonzalez Weekly Citizen*, October 5, 2021, https://www.weeklycitizen

.com/story/news/2021/10/05/ascension-parish-deputy-daniel-haydel -nominated-louisiana-sheriffs-association-valor-award/6006173001.

2. David J. Mitchell, "Ascension Deputy Had to 'Do Everything It Takes' to Rescue Family from Sinking Pickup," *The Advocate*, February 4, 2021, https://www.theadvocate.com/baton_rouge/news/article_20023a86-66fb -11eb-8b01-2bb327bf4358.html.

3. Every person is made in God's image. In my view, every person is *fully* an image-bearer, but Jesus Christ is *truly* the image of God (2 Corinthians 4:4). To understand this view, see Owen Strachan, *Reenchanting Humanity: A Theology of Mankind* (Fearn, Ross-Shire: Mentor, 2019), 27–32.

4. For more on Adam "guarding" Eden, see Raymond Ortlund, "Male-Female Equality and Male Headship," in *Recovering Biblical Manhood and Womanhood: A Response to Evangelical Feminism*, eds. John Piper and Wayne Grudem (Wheaton, Illinois: Crossway, 2006), 100.

5. It is not too much to say that this term "helper" (*ezer* in the Hebrew) is one of the Bible's most misunderstood words. It does not communicate inferiority in any way; it actually communicates the *opposite* idea, signaling that the woman has serious gifting and ability to offer the man as he leads the home. Andreas and Margaret Köstenberger point out that this word "is applied several times throughout the Old Testament to none other than God himself." See Exodus 18:4; Psalms 20:2, 33:20, and 146:5, among other texts. Andreas Köstenberger and Margaret Köstenberger, *God's Design for Man and Woman: A Biblical-Theological Survey* (Wheaton, Illinois: Crossway Books, 2014), 36.

6. We learn from Genesis here that there is no "gender spectrum," as we are told today. There is man and woman, two sexes, made by God. At the DNA level, there is XX (female) and XY (male). The concept of the "gender spectrum" does not owe to God or His Word; it owes to the magical gender thinking of the new paganism, and it must be summarily rejected as such.

7. To learn more on headship, see George W. Knight III, "Husbands and Wives as Analogues of Christ and the Church: Ephesians 5:21–33 and Colossians 3:18–19," in *Recovering Biblical Manhood and Womanhood: A Response to Evangelical Feminism*, eds. John Piper and Wayne Grudem (Wheaton, Illinois: Crossway, 2006), 170–71.

8. New Testament scholar Thomas Schreiner says it well. "The sway of death over all of humanity can be traced to Adam's sin. Whether human beings like it or not, we are one community. The fountainhead of the human race

affects all who come after him." Thomas R. Schreiner, *New Testament Theology: Magnifying God in Christ* (Grand Rapids, Michigan: Baker Academic, 2008), 538.

9. Confessing that all men are sinners is very different than claiming that all men are "toxic." Sin is a moral condition and can be overcome by God's redeeming kindness; toxicity is a therapeutic category and has no real antidote. Men can and do act wickedly and should be opposed in no uncertain terms for such acts. But men, like women (all of whom are sinners to their core), need the grace and mercy of God, not any therapeutic measure owing to secular psychology and philosophy. Further, even in their sin, men (like women) bear the image of God, which means that while they have fallen totally from Him, they nonetheless have been made by Him, have the live possibility of complete salvation, and still—even in their wretchedness—possess God-given dignity and worth.

10. To better understand the warrior dimension of Christ's life and death, see Owen Strachan, *The Warrior Savior: A Theology of the Work of Christ* (Phillipsburg, New Jersey: P&R, 2023).

Chapter 4: The Foundation of Manhood: Old Testament Men

1. Julie McEntee, private communication, January 8, 2022. I wrote about this effort on my Substack at https://owenstrachan.substack.com/p/boys-who-build-sheds-and-defy-low.

2. John MacArthur, "Gideon: A Weak Man Made Strong," message preached on Judges 6, September 7, 2015, Grace Community Church (Los Angeles), https://www.gty.org/library/blog/B150907/gideon-a-weak-man-made-strong.

3. Ibid.

4. Charles Spurgeon, "Shaven and Shorn, but Not beyond Hope," message preached on Judges 16:22, September 26, 1886, Metropolitan Tabernacle (London), https://www.spurgeon.org/resource-library/sermons/shaven-and-shorn-but-not-beyond-hope.

5. Grant Castleberry, "The Honor of God," 2022 sermon series, Capital Community Church (Raleigh), https://www.sermonaudio.com/solo/capitalcommchurch/sermons/series/160976.

6. To understand David in light of the whole Bible narrative, see Edmund Clowney, *The Unfolding Mystery: Discovering Christ in the Old Testament*, 2nd ed. (Phillipsburg, New Jersey: P&R, 2013).

Chapter 5: The Foundation of Strong Manhood: Jesus Christ

1. You can find more of this story in Owen Strachan and Gavin Peacock, *What Does the Bible Teach about Transgenderism?: A Short Book on Personal Identity*, Biblical Sexuality Series (Fearn, Ross-Shire: Christian Focus, 2020).

2. One can learn more about sound Christology through Stephen J. Wellum, *God the Son Incarnate: The Doctrine of Christ (Foundations of Evangelical Theology)* (Wheaton, Illinois: Crossway, 2016).

3. To glean more on the Spirit's empowerment of Jesus, see Bruce A. Ware, *The Man Christ Jesus: Theological Reflections on the Humanity of Christ* (Wheaton, Illinois: Crossway, 2012).

4. One excellent guide to the complex emotional life of Christ is B. B. Warfield, "The Emotional Life of Our Lord," https://www.monergism.com /thethreshold/articles/onsite/emotionallife.html.

5. For more on this crucial biblical theme, see Jonathan Edwards, "The Excellency of Christ (1738)," in *The Works of Jonathan Edwards*, ed. M. X. Lesser, vol. 19 (New Haven, Connecticut: Yale, 2001), 563–95.

Chapter 6: The Foundation of Strong Manhood: New Testament Teaching

1. Gillian Townsley, "Gender Trouble in Corinth: Que(e)rying Constructs of Gender in 1 Corinthians 11:2–16," *The Bible and Critical Theory* 2, no. 2 (2006): 17.7; see also Lewis Richard Farnell, *The Cults of the Greek States* (Oxford: Clarenden, 1909), 5:160.

2. A good resource on this count is Stuart Scott, *The Exemplary Husband: A Biblical Perspective* (Bemidji, Minnesota: Focus, 2002).

3. A helpful guide to creation order is found in Zachary M. Garris, *Masculine Christianity* (Ann Arbor, Michigan: Reformation Zion Publishing, 2020), 103–18.

4. For a biblical take on elders of the local church, consult Jeramie Rinne, *Church Elders: How to Shepherd God's People Like Jesus* (Wheaton, Illinois: Crossway, 2013).

5. Steven Lawson, "What Is Self-Discipline?," March 26, 2021, originally published in *Tabletalk* magazine, https://www.ligonier.org/posts/what-self -discipline.

Chapter 7: The Physical Distinctiveness of Men

1. For more on this condition, see J. Alan Branch, *Affirming God's Image: Addressing the Transgender Question with Science and Scripture* (Bellingham, Washington: Lexham, 2019). Steer well clear of resources that frame this matter as "intersex" and a matter of identity in a positive sense.

2. There are exceptional cases where a girl develops a womanly body but has male chromosomes. This is called complete androgen insensitivity syndrome (CAIS). To reiterate, the girl is indeed a girl, but develops male genitalia to a degree (usually undescended). According to Carole Hooven, this condition occurs in two out of 100,000 people. See Carole Hooven, *T: The Story of Testosterone, the Hormone that Dominates and Divides Us* (New York: Henry Holt, 2021), 50–54.

3. Lorenzo Jensen III, "14 Real Physical Differences between Men and Women (Besides the Obvious)," Thought Catalog, June 24, 2015, https://thoughtcatalog.com/lorenzo-jensen-iii/2015/06/14-real-physical-differences-between-men-and-women-besides-the-obvious.

4. Ibid.

5. Ibid.

6. Ibid.

7. Ibid.

8. David Geary, "Men's Advantages in Spatial Cognition and Mechanical Reasoning," *Psychology Today*, October 26, 2019, https://www.psychologytoday.com/us/blog/male-female/201910/men-s-advantages-in-spatial-cognition-mechanical-reasoning.

9. Ibid.

10. Anne and Bill Moir, *Why Men Don't Iron: The Fascinating and Unalterable Differences between Men and Women* (New York: Citadel, 1999), 221. Anne Moir is an Oxford-trained geneticist with a PhD in the field. This data compares favorably to unbiased scientific research from the Mayo Clinic: "Testosterone, Total, Bioavailable, and Free, Serum," Mayo Clinic Laboratories, accessed January 21, 2019, https://www.mayomedicallaboratories.com/test-catalog/Clinical+and+Interpretive/83686. One resource, reading the data from the Mayo Clinic, lists the average male-female testosterone ratios as follows: average level for an adult male, 270–1070 (ng/dl); average level for an adult female, 15–70. See Alexia Severson, "Testosterone Levels by Age," Healthline, https://www.healthline.com/health/low-testosterone/testosterone-levels-by-age.

11. Hooven, *T*, 9.

12. David J. Handelsman, Angelica L. Hirschberg, and Stephane Bermon, "Circulating Testosterone as the Hormonal Basis of Sex Differences in Athletic Performance," *Endocrine Reviews* 39, no. 5 (October 2018): 39:5, https://www.ncbi.nlm.nih.gov/pmc/articles/PMC6391653.

13. In the medical community, there is now a dispute over testosterone's role in manly behavior, a dispute that overlaps with the general challenge made today against the notion of biological sex. As one example, Hooven surfaces skepticism over traditional understandings of the role of testosterone in male lives—yet also notes of testosterone that "since it is responsible for making and maintaining male bodies (with a far smaller role in female ones)," it is appropriate to speak of testosterone as the "male sex hormone." She goes on to note that "pubertal boys have about thirty times as much T as girls." Hooven, *T*, 246.

14. Michael Gurian, *The Wonder of Boys: What Parents, Mentors and Educators Can Do to Shape Boys into Exceptional Men* (New York: Penguin, 2006), 9.

15. Ibid., 10.

16. Ibid.

17. Moir, *Why Men Don't Iron*, 173.

18. Ibid., 172.

Chapter 8: The Social Distinctiveness of Men

1. Channel 4 News, "Jordan Peterson Debate on the Gender Pay Gap, Campus Protests and Postmodernism," YouTube, January 16, 2018, https://www.youtube.com/watch?v=aMcjxSThD54.

2. Sometimes people will respond to a confession like this by saying, "Women should love Jesus, too! Why are you splitting up the sexes like this?" The reality is this: While men and women both need to love Jesus by God's grace, men always love Jesus—and practice all their faith—as men, just as women always love Jesus as women. We don't start our discipleship as men or women by blurring the sexes into a one-gender reality where we are not really distinctive. No, while recognizing the joyful reality of faith in Christ shared by both sexes, we always work out our faith as Christian men and Christian women. Many of our duties and callings overlap, but this does not obscure our calling as men and women. Further, as we have labored to show, God does have numerous instructions and duties to which He calls men, even as He does women. A proper biblical foundation for discipleship thus recognizes that the one true faith is to be lived out by Christian men

and Christian women. We start there and work outward, and avoid much confusion caused by neo-pagan androgyny.

Chapter 9: A Plan for Boys and a Way Back for Men

1. Ryan Michler, *The Masculinity Manifesto: How a Man Establishes Influence, Credibility, & Authority* (Washington, D.C.: Salem Books, 2022), xi.

2. Mike Fabarez, *Raising Men, Not Boys: Shepherding Your Sons to Be Men of God* (Chicago: Moody, 2017), 105–6.

3. Everyone, by the way, must sort out the gray areas of life as a man. Fathers, for example, have to guide their sons through all sorts of questions and situations that the Word of God does not directly address. We always stand on the doctrines and principles of the Word of God, but we all must use wisdom as best we can to shape our boys into men. Do boys play sports? If so, which ones? What jobs do they do? How do they dress? How do their household tasks differ from their sisters'? In these and many other ways, we see that we must use wisdom to raise our sons. But doing so will involve certain choices that others may not practice or adopt. That is fine, but all sides must see that those teaching their sons a brand of manhood are not unique; we all do this. Some will train their boys to be men in part by taking them hunting and fishing; others will train them by coaching them in football or soccer; others will do so by putting their sons to work in the family occupation. All these are valid training zones, and it is entirely appropriate to encourage other fathers to do the same, while also being clear that manhood is embodied and passed down through a range of approaches.